The Dz[illegible]

Innermost Essence Preliminary Practice

"Long-chen Nying-thig Ngön-dro"

with original Tibetan text

by

Jig-Me Ling-Pa

(1729-1798)

Translated with commentary by

Ven. Tulku Thondup

Edited by

Brian Beresford

LIBRARY OF TIBETAN WORKS AND ARCHIVES

First Edition: 1982
Second Revised edition: 1989
Third edition 1998
Fourth edition 2002

ISBN: 81-85102-19-8

Published by the Library of Tibetan Works and Archives, Dharamsala-176215, India, and printed at Indraprastha Press, New Delhi-110002.

Publisher's Note

It is with pleasure that we are able to introduce another text in our Bilingual series of translations. The Long-chen Nying-thig Ngondro is probably one of the most important liturgical texts for actual meditational practice found in the Nying-ma tradition. It is widely practiced and forms the basis for the introductory meditations of the Dzog-chen, or "Great Completeness" system of practices. Such texts are meant to be followed in close conjunction with direct instructions from a qualified spiritual master. It is supplemented by a concise commentary on the various aspects of the meditation and in the conclusion there is a lucid explanation of the Nying-ma system of dividing the Buddha's teachings into the Nine Spiritual Vehicles or yanas. Both Tulku Thondup and his editor, Brian Beresford, are to be commended for making this valuable translation available at this time of growing interest in the practice of Tibetan Buddhism. Special thanks are also due to Michael Richards for his excellent help and guidance in preparing the final manuscript for the press, and Ani-la Kelsang Chokyi for her assistance in typing and bringing the work to completion.

Gyatsho Tshering
Director

February 1982

Contents

Preface

The first part of this book is a direct translation of the liturgy on the Preliminary Practices of the Long-ch'en Nying-thig (Klong.chen. snying.thig.) tradition of the Great Completeness, or Dzog-ch'en (rdzogs.chen; mahāsandhi) teaching. The text is entitled The Excellent Path to Omniscience (rnam. mkhyen. lam. bzang) written by the All-knowing Jig-me-ling-pa ('jigs.med.gling.pa) (1729-1798), and compiled by the first Do-drub-ch'en (rdo.grub.chen) (1745-1821). Jig-me-ling-pa is considered the founder of the Long-ch'en Nying-thig tradition, and Do-drub-ch'en is looked upon as the principle holder of the doctrine. It is in effect a condensed practical handbook of Buddhism for followers of the Vajrayana school of Mahayana Buddhism. Its main subject, though not its sole concern, is the preliminary practices or that which "goes before" (sngon. 'gro) the actual practice. However, this is somewhat misleading, since it also contains a complete course of practice for achieving Buddhahood itself.

A line by line translation of the full text has been prepared and precedes the Tibetan root text. A few sub-headings have been added for clarity, but these have been placed in parentheses.

The second part of the book is summation of the liturgy, giving a brief yet comprehensive explanation of the method of practice. this summary draws upon instructions I have received from my principle Lamas and from the following texts:

1. Kun.bzang.bla.ma'i.zhal.lung. by sPal.sprul.Rin.po.ch'e.
2. Khrid.yig.dran.pa.nyer.bzhag.by Kun.mkhyen.'Jigs.med.gLing.pa.
3. rNam.mkhyen.lam.bzang.gsal.byedby mKhyen.brtse'i.dbang.po.
4. Thar.lam.gsal.byed.sgron.me. by 'Gro.'dul.dPa.bo.rdo.rje.
5. Rig.'dzin.zhal.lung. by mKhan.po.ch'e mch'og.don.grub.

The third part of the book contains a brief outline of the Nine Vehicles of the Nying-ma (rnying.ma) school on the basis of the books of Long-ch'en-pa, Jig-me-ling-pa and others. The kind and able assistance of Mr. Pema Lodro Gyatsho made it possible for me to render this work into English, and thereby make this small book available to its readers. I am greatly indebted to him. I also gratefully acknowledge my thanks to Mr. Pema Thrinley Gyathso and other members of the Buddhayana Foundation, United States of America, for sponsoring the preparation and translation of several works, including this one, in the United States.

Thanks to Ani-la Kelsang Chokyi (Dee) for her assistance in typing and bringing this work to completion.

My thanks also go to Mr. Gyatsho Tshering, the Director of the Library of Tibetan Works and Archives, Dharamsala, for sponsoring the publication of this book. My appreciation also goes to Brian Beresford for his assistance and his work on editing the entire manuscript.

Tulku Thondup
Visva-Bharati University,
Shantiniketan1977

Introduction

There are many different methods of teaching the Dharma that were expounded by the Buddha, the realized saints who followed after him in India and Tibet, and the traditional scholars. All of these are for the benefit of disciples of differing capabilities. For the practice of Dharma to be effective one should start at a level suited to one's own mental capacity. It is essential to understand the meaning of the teaching first of all through study. Trying to practice it without having studied it properly would be like trying to scale a cliff without hands. Conversely, a great deal of study and no practice would be like being surrounded by an abundance of food while dying of hunger. it is important, therefore, for the practice of Dharma to combine both understanding its meaning and trying to realize it through practice.

This text, the Dzog-chen Long-chen Nying-thig, belongs to the category of "Dharma Treasures" (gTer.chos) and the writings of the All-knowing Master, Jig-me Ling-pa. The tradition of the Long-chen Nying-thig in Tibet became very popular, and was a widely studied and practiced system within the Nyingmapa tradition, one of the four major Buddhist sects in Tibet. The Long-chen Nying-thig is a relatively new system, even though the teachings and the practices are basically the same as the earlier Dzog-chen Nying-thig, which was brought to Tibet about the time of Guru Rinpoche, Padmasambhava, in the eighth century. The lineages of transmission of the Dzog-chen Nying-thig and the Long-chen Nying-thig are as follows:

1. The Dzog-chen Nying-thig Lineage

According to the tradition of the Nyingma school, Tibet's earliest, the highest teaching is known as the Great Completion, or Dzog-pa Chen-po (rdzogs.chen; mahāsaṃpatra or mahāshāndi), or the Atiyoga direct method for realizing the nature of the mind and attaining Buddhahood. The Nying-thig, or the "Essence of the

Heart" teachings, precisely explain the various methods for directly actualizing the innermost teachings of the Dzog-pa Chen-po. The Dzog-chen Nying-thig, as a teaching, fundamentally deals with the expression of the doctrine of the Three Kayas, or the Three Perfect Bodies of a Fully Awakened Being, and they have arisen through the three systems of spiritual transmission.

The first is known as the Mind Transmission of the Buddhas. In this system the teacher transmits the teachings to a disciple without using words or any other indication. The disciple attains a state of union with the teacher like a reflection of the moon in the still water, which mirrors a perfect likeness of the moon itself. This level of spiritual transmission is from the Primordial Buddha, Kun-tu Zang-po (kun.tu.bzang.po; Samantabhadra), on the level of the Dharmakāya, or Perfect Body of Truth. The Dzog-chen teachings are then passed on through the level of the Saṃbhogakāya, the Perfect Body of Enjoyment, which includes the Five Dhyāni Buddhas on the level of pure mystic vision.

The second level of spiritual transmission is known as the Knowledge-holders' Indication system. Here, a Knowledge-holder (rig.'dzin; vidyadhāra), a being who has direct and pure vision of the nature of reality, manifests to a receptive disciple and transmits the teaching by means of pronouncing a mantra or showing a sign. In this case the Saṃbhogakāya Being, Vajrasattva, mystically appeared before the Indian teacher Prahevajra who existed on the level of the Nirmāṇakāya, or Perfect Body of Manifestation, and in one instant transmitted all empowerments and instructions so that Prahevajra spontaneously and effortlessly attained Enlightenment. He in turn transmitted the teachings to his disciple Mañjushrīmitra, who passed them on to Shrīsiṅha. Shrīsiṅha transmitted his insight to Jñānasūtra, Vimalamitra and Padmasambhava, or Guru Rinpoche, the Indian Tantric saint who later brought them into Tibet. Vimalamitra also received his teachings from Prāmodhavajra and Mañjushrīmitra, and Padmasaṃbhava himself also received the teaching directly from Mañjushrīmitra.

The third system of spiritual transmission of the Dzog-chen lineage is that known as the Audial Transmission of the Yogis. In this system the complete verbal empowerment and instructions are transmitted by word of mouth from practitioner to practitioner. This form of spiritual transmission in Tibet initially spread through two lineages in the beginning and the early part of the ninth century. One originates from Vimalamitra, the other from Guru

Rinpoche. Vimalamitra transmitted the teachings in Tibet to Nyag Ting-dzin Zang-po and King Tri-song De-tsen and other disciples. From Nyag this unbroken lineage of audial transmission came down to Long-chen Rab-jam, and through various spiritually realized teachers. The other lineage, from Guru Rinpoche, was passed on to his disciple, the Ḍākinī Yeshe Tso-gyal and Princess Pema-säl. The texts for these teachings were mystically concealed by Guru Rinpoche, to be unearthed later for the benefit of his disciples. These were later discovered by a male incarnation of the Princess, the teacher Pema Lä-tro-tsal, and in his next incarnation as Long-chen Rab-jam-pa. He expounded these teachings together with extraordinary commentaries.

The Innermost Essence teachings through the first lineage are known as the Vimala Nying-thig, and the second are known as the Kha-dro Nying-thig. In this way both of these Innermost Essence transmissions meet in Long-chen Rab-jam-pa, who lived from 1308-1363. From him the uninterrupted audial transmission of these teachings have extended until the present day.

The three systems outlined above are divided here in a very general way. There were also numerous mystical saints and practitioners, both in India and Tibet, who received or gave teachings through the Mind or Indication spiritual transmissions.

2. The Dzog-chen Long-chen Nying-thig Lineage

In the eighteenth century the spiritual master Jig-me Ling-pa (1729-1798), a reincarnation of the king Tri-song De-tsen, received the complete Dzog-chen Nying-thig teachings in a mystical vision from Mañjushrīmitra, Guru Rinpoche, Vimalamitra, and Long-chen Rab-jam-pa, through Mind, the Indication and the Audial transmissions, in the state of pure vision. In these visions he saw Long-chen Rab-jam-pa three times, received the blessings of being inseparable from the Spiritual Master and thereby the true state of Perfect Accomplishment, or Buddhahood. He discovered the "Concealed Treasures of Dharma" (gter.chos) of the Long-chen Nying-thig, and thus founded this tradition. The Dzog-chen Nying-thig and the Long-chen Nying-thig are also known respectively as the Earlier and Later Nying-thig teachings. The lineage of Audial transmission through which these have reached my teacher, the Fourth Do-drub-chen Rinpoche, is as follows:

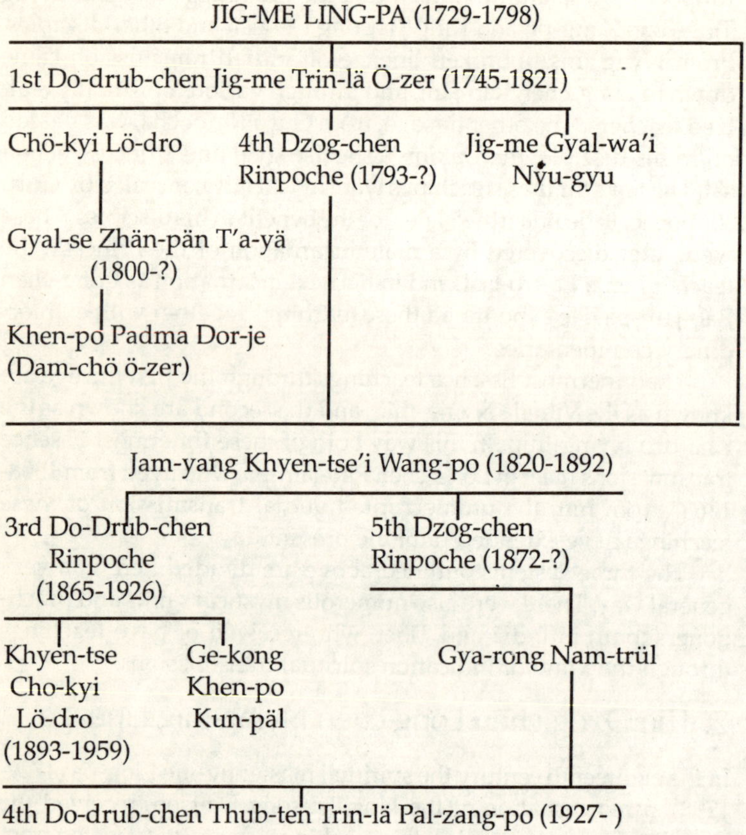
JIG-ME LING-PA (1729-1798)
1st Do-drub-chen Jig-me Trin-lä Ö-zer (1745-1821)
Chö-kyi Lö-dro
4th Dzog-chen Rinpoche (1793-?)
Jig-me Gyal-wa'i Nyu-gyu
Gyal-se Zhän-pän T'a-yä (1800-?)
Khen-po Padma Dor-je (Dam-chö ö-zer)
Jam-yang Khyen-tse'i Wang-po (1820-1892)
3rd Do-Drub-chen Rinpoche (1865-1926)
5th Dzog-chen Rinpoche (1872-?)
Khyen-tse Cho-kyi Lö-dro (1893-1959)
Ge-kong Khen-po Kun-päl
Gya-rong Nam-trül
4th Do-drub-chen Thub-ten Trin-lä Pal-zang-po (1927-)

Part -I

The Excellent Path of Omniscience

The Preliminary Practices of Long-chen-pa's "Innermost Essence for the Great Completion: Dzog-pa Chen-po"

Tibetan
rDzogs-pa chen-po kLong-chen snying-thig sngon-'gro

Composed by
The Knowledge-holding master
Jig-me Ling-pa

Compiled by
The first Do-drub-chen Rinpoche, Jig-me Trin-lä Wö-zer

Homage

You who have attained Buddhahood primordially but have never ceased appearing as the perfect body of form (rūpakāya) for whomsoever is receptive to it;
Exhibiting various illusory manifestations yet free from both the grasping mind and its object, the body-mind constituents, sensory spheres and bases;
Appearing in human form while in fact a Buddha, radiating thousands of light rays comprising wisdom and compassion;
I depend on you for firm refuge not simply for this life but forever; bestow your blessings upon me.

Preliminaries of Long-chen-pas "Innermost Essence for the Great Completion" in eleven parts:

1. Prayer Invoking the Mind-stream of the Gracious Lama

O Lama! O Lama! O Lama!

[Having invoked the presence of the Lama with intense devotion, recite the following:]

From the blossoming lotus of devotion at the center of my heart
Sole protector, gracious Lama, arise!
For my protection against misfortune,
From torment by the vicious legacy of actions and defilements
Be enshrined as the ornament in the Wheel of Great Bliss on the crown of my head;
Let there arise in me total recollection and mindfulness.

[The rarity of a human rebirth characterized by eight freedoms and ten endowments.]

At this time, I have gained this leisure free from the eight kinds of bondage:
From hell, hungry ghost and animal realms;
From the realms of the long-lived gods, barbarians and perverse philosophers;
From being a fool, from a place in which no Buddha has appeared.
To have been born a human being complete with sensory faculties, in a central land congenial to Dharma,
Not to have reverted to extreme wrong deeds and to have faith in the Buddhist teachings;

These comprise the five personal endowments.
When a Buddha has appeared,
Has expounded the truth of Dharma,
When the teachings survive and are being followed,
And when one has been accepted by a spiritual friend; these are the five circumstantial endowments,
Which, despite my possessing them completely, may become wasted in this life
By uncertain circumstances,
Giving cause for birth into this transitory world again.
O Guru Rinpoche, turn my mind towards the Dharma.
Long-chen-pa and Jig-me-ling-pa, exalted and all-knowing, let me not deviate into any wrong and inferior path.
O Lama, you who are one with them:
Hear me!

If this present opportunity to practice Dharma is not taken seriously,
In the future this basis for achieving liberation will not be regained.
Once the merits that gave cause for this happy existence have been consumed,
I will wander after death as an inferior being through the lower realms.
Unable to differentiate virtue from non-virtue I will not hear the sound of Dharma,
Nor will I meet with a virtuous spiritual friend—indeed a great disaster.
Merely to think about the numberless variety of sentient beings
Is to realize that obtaining a human body is just barely possible.
To see mankind doing non-virtue, irreligious acts,
Is to realize that those who act spiritually are as rare as stars in broad daylight.
O Guru Rinpoche, turn my mind towards the Dharma.
All-knowing Long-chen-pa and exalted Jig-me-ling-pa, let me not deviate into any wrong and inferior path.
O Lama, you who are one with them:
Hear me!

[The eight unfree states caused by temporal events]

Even had I arrived at this jewel island, the human form,
An impoverished mind in such an auspicious body
Could not be a basis befitting the accomplishment of liberation.
Especially: to be entrapped by harmful influences or polluted by the five poisons,
To be struck by the lightening of non-virtue Karma or to be distracted by laziness,
To be enslaved by others, to practice Dharma as a defence from fear or with pretension,
Or to be thick-headed and the like, are the eight unfree states caused by temporal events.
When these utter contradictions to Dharma are visited upon me,
O Guru Rinpoche, turn my mind towards the Dharma.
All-knowing Long-chen-pa and exalted Jig-me-ling-pa, let me not deviate into any wrong and inferior path.
O Lama, you who are one with them:
Hear me!

[The eight unfree states caused by mental aberration]

To lack remorse and the jewel of faith,
To be bound by the lasso of desire and greed or to behave crudely,
Not to refrain from unskillful and non-virtue actions, or to live by dishonest means,
To undermine one's vows and rend precepts asunder;
These are the eight unfree states caused by mental aberration.
O Guru Rinpoche, turn my mind towards the Dharma.
All-knowing Long-chen-pa and exalted Jig-me-ling-pa, let me not deviate into any wrong and inferior path.
O Lama, you who are one with them:
Hear me!

[Impermanence of life]

At present I am not tormented by sufferings and illness.
I have not come under the control of others, such as being a slave.

So while I have this opportunity of independence,
If I waste the fortunate human life by idleness,
No question of retinue, wealth, or relations,
But this very body which I cherished
Will be removed from bed and taken to a deserted place,
To be eaten by foxes, vultures and dogs,
At that time,
In the Bardo, I will feel terrible fear:
O Guru Rinpoche, turn my mind towards the Dharma.
All-knowing Long-chen-pa and exalted Jig-me-ling-pa, let me not deviate into any wrong and inferior path.
O Lama, you who are one with them:
Hear me!

[Karma: the cause and result of action]

The result of non-virtue and virtuous Karmas will follow after me.

[The suffering of saṃsara]

Especially if I am born in the realm of hell,
On a ground of burning iron my body and head will be cut by instruments,
Split by saws and crushed by burning hammers.
I will cry for help, suffocating in a doorless (burning) iron house.
Pierced by burning spears and boiled in molten iron
I will burn in extremely hot fire—the eight (hot hells).
Amid snow mountains and freezing cold water,
In a place of terrible distress and fear, I will be blasted by blizzards.
Beaten by very cold winds, my flesh will have
Blisters, glaring wounds.
I will bewail without ceasing, and
By these feelings of unbearable suffering,
Like a sick and dying man whose strength is exhausted,
I will experience gasping, clenching of teeth, and the cracking of the skin,
Flesh emerging from the wounds, broad cracks of the skin: the eight (cold hells).
Likewise I shall experience being cut on a field of razors,

My body cut in pieces in a forest of swords;
Trapped in disgusting mud; suffering in an expanse of unfordable hot ashes:
The sub-hells and the changing hells.
Trapped in doors, pillars, stoves, ropes, etc.
Always used and exploited: the scattered hells.
When the cause of these 18 Hells—
Powerful angry thoughts—arises,
O Guru Rinpoche, turn my mind towards the Dharma.
All-knowing Long-chen-pa and exalted Jig-me-ling-pa, let me not deviate into any wrong and inferior path.
O Lama, you who are one with them:
Hear me!

[The suffering of the hungry ghosts]

In a poor and unpleasant land
Where the names of wealth, food, and drink had never been known,
Food and drink cannot be found for months and years.
The bodies of hungry ghosts
Are very feeble, and they are too exhausted to stand up: the three types of hungry ghosts.
The cause of their arising is miserliness.

[The suffering of animals]

In great fear of death by being eaten by one another,
Exhausted by servitude and ignorant of what is good and bad to do.
Being tormented by endless sufferings,
Of which the seed is the darkness of ignorance in which I am wandering.
O Guru Rinpoche, turn my mind towards the Dharma.
All-knowing Long-chen-pa and exalted Jig-me-ling-pa, let me not deviate into any wrong and inferior path.
O Lama, you who are one with them:
Hear me!

[Recognizing one's own faults]

I have entered the path of Dharma but do not restrain my wrong conduct.

I have entered the door of the Mahayana, but lack the thought of the benefit of others.
I have received the Four Empowerments but am not practicing the Developing and Perfecting Stages.
O Lama, protect me from this errant path.
Though the view is not realized, I act in a crazy manner;
Though meditation wavers, I cling to hearsay;
Though my conduct is wrong, I ignore my faults;
O Lama, protect me from indifference to Dharma.
Even if death comes tomorrow, I covet a house, clothes, and wealth.
Even though youth has long since passed away, I lack renunciation and revulsion,
Although little Dharma has been studied, I boast about my scholarship,
O Lama, protect me from this ignorance.
Although they lead me into (harmful) circumstances,
I wish for entertainments and pilgrimages,
Although I stay in solitary places, the ordinary mind remains rigid like a tree.
I talk about discipline but do not eradicate desire and hatred.
O Lama, protect me from these eight (worldly) Dharmas.
Let me awaken quickly from this thick sleep.
Swiftly pull me out of this dark prison.
[Thus invoke strongly the compassion of the Guru.]

2. Refuge

To the actual three rare and supreme Jewels,[1] those Gone to Bliss[2] to the Three Roots,[3]
To the nature of (physical) channels, energy and essence,[4]
To the maṇḍala of the essence, nature and compassion of the Awakening Mind,[5]
I go for refuge until the attainment of the quintessence of awakening.[6]
[repeat three times]

3. Activating the Awakening Mind

Deceived by myriad appearances like the moon's reflection in water,
Sentient beings wander through the cyclic chain of lives;
So they may be at ease[7] in the luminescent expanse of intrinsic awareness,[8]
I shall activate the Awakening Mind, contemplating on the four boundless states.[9]
[repeat three times]

4. Meditation and Recitation of Vajrasattva

i. The visualization

AH:
In my ordinary form; above my head
Is a white lotus with a lunar seat in its fold:
From a HŪṂ above this arises the Lama as Vajrasattva
White, translucent, the perfect body of complete enjoyment,[10]
Holding a vajra and bell and embracing his consort.

ii. Petition

I request your protection; purify my negativities.
With intense regret I confess and acknowledge;
Even at the cost of my life I shall abstain.

iii. Purification

Upon a full moon in your heart
Is the letter HŪṂ encircled by the mantra.
By invoking with the recitation of mantras
From the point of union of the deities' blissful play
Flows nectar-clouds of bodhichitta
Falling like fine particles of camphor.

iv. Requesting

I implore you to utterly purify
Myself and all beings throughout the three realms[11]
Of our Karma and conflicting emotions, the cause of suffering,

As well as illness, harmful spirits, negativities, mental obscurations and transgressions of vows.

v. Mantra recitation

OM VAJRA SATTVA SAMAYA/MANU PĀLAYA/VAJRA SATTVA
TVENO PATIṢHṬHṬA/DṚḌHO ME BHĀVA/SUTOSH-YOME BHĀVA/
SUPOṢHYO ME BHĀVA/ANURAKTO ME BHĀVA/SARVA SIDDHIMME PRAYACHCHHA/SARVA
KARMA SUCHA ME/CHITTAM SHRIYAMH KURU HŪṂ/ HA HA HA HA HOḤ
BHAGAVĀN/SARVA TATHĀGATA/VAJRA MĀ ME MUÑCHA/VAJRI
BHĀVA/MAHĀSAMAYA SATTVA/Ā
[recite as much as possible]

vi. Invocation and dissolving the visualization

O Protector, through my lack of knowledge and ignorance
I have transgressed and weakened the sacred pledges;
O Lama, Protector, give me refuge.
Lord, Vajradhara, holder of the adamantine scepter
Whose very nature is great compassion,
The lord of beings, to you I go for refuge.

I confess and acknowledge all transgressions of the root and branch commitments done physically, verbally and mentally. Please purify and cleanse away all strains of wrongdoings, emotional obscurations, errors and downfalls.

At these words, Vajrasattva, with a glad and smiling countenance says, "O fortunate child, all your wrongdoings, obscurations and transgressions are purified." So saying he merges into radiant light and dissolves into me. By this means I become Vajrasattva, apparent yet empty, like a reflection in a mirror. By visualizing the heart-syllable HŪṂ encircled by four letters, light rays are emitted so that all beings are the realms of the three worlds become perfected in the nature of awakened beings, Vajrasattva, the five Buddha families, maṇḍalas and retinues.

OṂ VAJRASATTVA HŪṂ
[reciting as much as possible remain in meditative equipoise]

5. Maṇḍala Offering

OṂ—ĀḤ—HŪṂ!

i. Nirmānakāya maṇḍala

A billion universes encompassing the three-thousand worlds
Filled with the wealth of gods and men and the seven precious jewels,
I offer in its entirety together with my body and possessions
That I may attain the state of a Dharma-ruler of the universe.

ii. Saṃbhogakāya maṇḍala

By offering the ultimately blissful, beautifully arrayed pure realm of Akanishṭha,
With assemblies of the five Buddha families endowed with the five certainties,
And inconceivable billowing clouds of offerings comprising the sensory objects,
May I enjoy the Buddha field of the perfect body of enjoyment—the Saṃbhogakāya.

iii. Dharmakāya maṇḍala

By offering utterly pure phenomenal appearances, the perfect body of the vase of immortality (eternal youth),
Embellished by unimpeded compassion, and the play of Reality Itself,
Together with the utterly pure apprehension of perfect form and energy,
May I delight in the Buddha field of the perfect body of truth—the Dharmakāya.

6. The Yogi-mendicant's Accumulation of Merit

Phaṭ!
By throwing out cherishing the body, the demon of the gods is destroyed.
The mind is shot out into the pure expanse through the fontanel,

Destroying the demon of death and becoming Rudrāni[12]
(the yoginī)
Who wields the curved vajra blade in her right hand,
which slays the demon of the conflicting emotions.
I annihilate the demon of the bodily aggregation by cutting off my skull;
My left hand actively wrenches away the head
And places it upon a tripod stove of three human heads,
symbolizing the three perfect bodies.
In it is my corpse which fills the three-thousand-fold
universes;
The short ĀḤ and HŪṂ syllables melt the corpse into the
nectar;
By the power of the three letters (OṂ, ĀḤ and HŪṂ dissolving into the offering), it is purified, increased and
transformed.
OṂ ĀḤ HŪṂ!
[after reciting many times:]

Phaṭ!
The wishes of the upper guests of offering are fulfilled
The accumulations are perfected, and the common and
uncommon attainments are achieved.
The lower guests of saṃsāra are satisfied and their debts
are paid.
Especially the harmful and obstructive spirits are satisfied
Illness, evil spirits, and obstacles are pacified into empty
space.
Harmful circumstances and clinging to self are blasted
to atoms.
Finally all the offering, offerer, and object of offering
Dissolve into unmodified Dzog-pa Chen-po—Āh!

7. Unification with the Spiritual Master (Guru Yoga)

i. Visualization

E—MA—HO!
My perceptions spontaneously arise as the absolute pure
realms,
The perfectly arrayed Glorious Copper-colored Mountain. In the center

Is my own body but now as Vajra Yoginī's;
Red and translucent, with one face and two hands, holding the curved vajra blade and skull-cup of blood.
My two legs are placed in the "advancing posture" and my three eyes gaze up into space.
Upon my head on an unfolding hundred-thousand-petalled lotus,
Seated upon a sun and a moon, is the perfect emanation body
Of Padmasaṃbhava, Saroruha Vajra,
The synthesis of all objects of refuge and inseparable from my Root Lama.
His complexion is white with pinkish hue and he is youthful in appearance.
He is attired in a gown, a monastic robe and brocade cape,
Has one face, two arms and sits in the playful posture of a king.
In his right hand he holds a vajra scepter, in the left a skull-cup containing a vase of immortality.
He wears the lotus hat on his head,
And in the cleft of his left arm is the divine consort of bliss and emptiness
Concealed in the form of the sacred Khaṭvaṅga trident.
He sits amidst radiant rainbows, light rays and shimmering nuclei of light;
In the outer perimeters, in the expanse of an exquisite lattice of five-colored light,
Are seated the 25 emanation disciples,
The spiritual scholars, realized sages,
Knowledge-holders, divine meditational deities,
The Ḍākinīs and Dharma protectors, all gathered like billowing clouds;
They are perceived in the state of great equipoise of luminescence and emptiness.

ii. Invitation

HŪṂ!
In the northwest country of Uddiyāna
Is the one (born) on the pistil stem of a lotus
And endowed with supreme marvelous attainments;

Renowned as the Lotus Born One, Padmasaṃbhava,
and surrounded by a retinue of many ḍākinīs.
I will practice by following you;
Please come forth to grace me with your inspiration.
GURU PADMA SIDDHI HŪṂ:

iii. The Seven Aspects of Devotional Practice

(A) HOMAGE AND PROSTRATION

By projecting my body to equal the atoms
In the universe I prostrate in homage to you.

(B) OFFERING

Offerings actually arrayed and those mentally emanated by the power of meditation—
I present phenomenal existence to you in the mode of an offering.

(C) CONFESSION

All unwholesome actions I have committed through my three doors,[13]
I openly declare within the state of the radiant clarity of the Dharmakāya.

(D) REJOICING

I rejoice in the entire accumulation of merit
Which is contained within the two realities.

(E) REQUESTING THE CYCLE OF DHARMA TO BE TAUGHT

I request you to set into motion
The cycle of Dharma of the Three Vehicles.

(F) BESEECHING THE REALIZED BEINGS TO REMAIN ALIVE

Until cyclic existence is emptied
Please remain, pass not into the state beyond sorrow.

(G) DEDICATION

All merit accumulated throughout the three times
I dedicate for the cause of great awakening, the state of pristine consummation.

iv. Invocation

O venerable lord, Guru Rinpoche:
You are the synthesis of the compassionate
Inspiration of all fully awakened beings.
To you who are the sole protector of all beings
I offer my body, possessions, mind,
Heart and soul without reservation.
From now until my complete awakening,
Through all happiness and pain, good and bad, heights and depths,
I will rely upon you venerable lord, Padmasaṃbhava:
No others are there to rely on,
For transmigrating beings in this degenerate time
Are sinking in the swamp of unending misery.
O great Guru, protect us from this;
Blessed One, bestow the four empowerments;
Compassionate One, develop our understanding;
Powerful One, purify our dual obscurations.

When the end of my life comes about
May appearances be perceived as the realm of the Glorious Mountain, Cāmara Shrīparvata, in which
May my body be transformed into Vajrayoginī,
Translucent and brilliantly radiant,
In that pure realm of the Emanation of Total Integration.
There may I attain Buddhahood as totally inseparable
From the venerable lord, Padmasaṃbhava.
Out of the display of the great primordial awareness
Which is the manifestation of bliss and emptiness,
Inspire me, Sublime Guru Rinpoche,
To be the supreme Spiritual Master who guides
All sentient beings of the three realms.
I pray from the very depths of my heart,
Not merely mouthing these words alone,
That you bless me with inspiration from the vast expanse of your mind
That all these aspiration may be fulfilled.

v. Recitation of the mantra

OṂ ĀḤ HŪṂ VAJRA GURU PADMA SIDDI HŪṂ
(O Padma, weighty with vajra qualities and the three sacred things, bestow inspirational blessings).

8. Prayers to the Lamas of the Lineage

E—MA-HO!
In the Pure Land free from partiality and limitations,
The primordial Dharmakāya Buddha Samantabhadra;
The Saṃbhogakāya Vajrasattva arisen like the moon in water;
Prahevajra fully endowed as the Nirmāṇakāya;
I pray to you to bestow the blessing and empowerment upon us.

Treasure of the ultimate doctrine, Shrisiṅha;
Universal king of the Nine Yānas, Mañjushrīmitra;
Jñanāsūtra and great scholar Vimalamitra,
To you I pray: show us the way to liberation.

The sole ornament of the Jambu continent, Padmasaṃbhava;
The true, excellent heart-sons, the Lord, the subjects, and the friend,
Revealer of the symbols of oceans like Mind-treasures, Long-chen Rab-jam,
Entrusted with the treasure of the sphere of the Ḍākinīs, Jig-me Ling-pa;
I pray to you, bestow the accomplishment and liberation.

Additional Prayers to the Lamas of the Lineage

Scholar and Siddha, Kun-Zang Zhän-phän-päl,
Lotus-holder Gyal-wa'i Nyu-gu,
The very Mañjushrī, great Khen-po named Padma,
To you I pray: show me the self-identity of the nature.
Especially, of the profound luminescent Nying-thig,
The great chariot, Do-ngag Ling-pa,
Root Lama of unequalled preciousness
To you I pray, enable us spontaneously to achieve the two-fold purpose.

Aspirational Prayers

(A) ASPIRATIONS FOR THIS LIFE

Out of the detachment leading to the definite intention to transcend worldly existence,

May I rely upon my Vajra-Lama as I do upon my eyes;
By profoundly taking to heart whatever he instructs me to do.
With intense and diligent consistency, never letting up,
May the inspiration of your mind's profound vision be transferred to me.

Since all phenomenal appearances, saṃsāra and nirvāṅa, from the very beginning are the pure realm of Akaniṣhṭha,
They are consequently perfected,[13] purified and ripened into divinities, mantras and the Dharmakāya;
Great Completeness, Dzog-chen, is free from the efforts of abandoning or adopting;
The depth of intrinsic awareness[15] is beyond mental fabrication and known experience;
May I nakedly see Reality Itself[16] in direct actuality.[17]

From within the depths of the rainbow radiance, utterly freed from characteristic thoughts,
May I develop the visionary experience of pure forms and light discs, and
Perfect the play of intrinsic awareness[18] into the Saṃbhogakāya pure realm.
May I become fully awakened in the great transcendence, the dissolution of phenomena, and
Gain the stronghold of the youthful vase-body.

(B) ASPIRATIONS FOR THE INTERMEDIATE (BARDO) STATE

If I do not succeed in experiencing the great yoga,
And my gross body is not released into the subtle expanse (of the rainbow body),
Then when the life functions are collapsing,
May death's clear-light vision arise as the primordially pure perfect body of truth,
And may the apparitions of the intermediate state be liberated into the perfect body of complete enjoyment.
Once the skills of the path of total decisiveness[19] and spontaneous presence[20] have been perfected,
May I attain liberation like a child climbing upon it's mothers lap.

(C) ASPIRATIONS FOR THE FUTURE REBIRTH

If I were not released into the primordial state where one actualizes
The face of the Dharmakāya, which is not to be sought other than in
The great esoteric luminescence, the summit of the Supreme Vehicle,
Then may I fully awaken, without meditation,through the excellent path of the five practices,[21]
Attaining the five pure realms[22] of the natural Nirmāṇakāya
And especially the radiant Palace of the Lotus,[23]
Where joyous celebrations of the sacred esoteric doctrine are held
By the supreme leader of the ocean-like
Knowledge-Holders, the glorious Orgyen Rinpoche.
May I, in being born as his finest spiritual disciple, be spiritually elevated
And fulfill the needs of limitless transmigrating beings.

(D) THE PRAYER TO ACHIEVE THESE ASPIRATIONS

By the inspiration of the ocean-like Knowledge-holders
And the might of the truth of the Expanse of Reality,
The Dharmadhātu that cannot be encompassed by thought—
May I, with the leisure and opportunities of this human life, realize the interdependent relationship of the threefold
Process of perfecting, maturing and purifying[24] and attain the fully awakened state of being.
[Pray thus from the heart.]

9. Receiving the Four Empowerments

i. The Vase Empowerment

From the mid-forehead of Guru Rinpoche a white OṂ, shimmering like crystal, radiates light rays
Which penetrate the crown of my head,
Cleansing (contaminated) actions of the body and impediments of the channel system

Instilling blessing of the Vajra-body
So that I obtain the Empowerment of the Vase,
Becoming a fitting vessel for the visualization process;
The seed of a yet-to-mature Knowledge-holder is sown,
And in my mind is placed the capacity for attaining the state of the emanation body, the Nirmāṇakāya.

ii. The Secret Empowerment

From the throat (of Guru Rinpoche) a letter ĀḤ, blazing like a lotus ruby, radiates light rays
Which penetrate my throat,
Purifying verbal actions and impediments of energy;
Instilling blessing of the Vajra-speech
So that I receive the Secret Empowerment,
Becoming receptive for the (mystic) recitation.
The seed for maturation of a Knowledge-holder of Immortality is sown,
And in my mind is placed the capacity for attaining the state of the perfect body of complete enjoyment, the Saṃbhogakāya.

iii. The Primordial Wisdom Empowerment

From the heart (of Guru Rinpoche) a letter HŪṂ, the color of the sky, radiates light rays
Which penetrate my heart,
Purifying mental actions and impediments of essence—the "thig-le";
Instilling blessings of the Vajra-mind
So that I obtain the Primordial Wisdom Empowerment,
Becoming a fitting vessel for the heat[25] practice of bliss and emptiness.
The seed of a Knowledge-holder of the Mudrā is sown,
And in my mind is placed the capacity for attaining the state of the perfect body of truth, the Dharmakāya.

iv. The Verbal Indication Empowerment

Again from the HŪṂ in (Guru Rinpoche's) heart, a second letter HŪṂ bursts forth like a meteor
Mixing indistinguishably with my mind,
Purifying actions of the universal foundation[26] and instinctive obscurations;[27]

Instilling blessing of the Vajra-primordial Wisdom
So that I obtain the ultimate empowerment indicated by words,
Becoming a fitting vessel for the primordially pure Great Completeness;
The seed of a Knowledge-holder of spontaneous accomplishment is sown,
And in my mind is placed the capacity for the final attainment, the perfect body of universal essence, the Svabhāvakāya.
(By integrating the meditation with this recitation, complete the receiving of the empowerments).

v. Dissolving the visualization

(Finally), from the heart of the Lama, rays of warm red light are emitted and just by touching the heart of myself as translucent Vajrayoginī, I become a sphere of red light which dissolves into the heart of Guru Rinpoche, mixing inseparably, meditating on becoming as "one taste".
(Remain in this essential equipoise devoid of conceptuality, thought or expression)

vi. Prayer to the Lama

O Glorious Root Lama, precious one,
Dwell on the lotus-seat in my heart,
Look upon me and care for me out of your great kindness,
And grant me the actualization of your body, speech and mind.

Regarding the activities of my glorious Root Lama,
May I never develop a wrong view for even a moment,
And by the respect in observing whatever he does as good,
May my Lama's inspirational blessings enter my mind.

Through all successive lifetimes may I never be apart
From perfect Lamas, and may I enjoying the wondrous Dharma,
Perfect the qualities of the spiritual stages and paths,
And swiftly attain the state of Vajradhara.

10. Dedication

By this virtue may all beings
Complete the accumulation of merit and wisdom,
Attaining the two supreme perfect bodies
That arise from merit and primordial wisdom.

Whatever virtue is possessed by beings
And by whatever virtuous actions they have done, will do and likewise are doing,
May all beings, by all means, achieve
The stages to perfection, as Samantabhadra did.

Just as the Boddhisattva Mañjushrī gained wisdom,
And Samantabhadra, too,
I dedicate these virtuous entirely (to the welfare of all)
So that I may train myself to follow them.

By all the Victors of the three times who have gone beyond;
The dedication of merits has been greatly praised.
Therefore, these virtues of myself also
I shall dedicate for the purpose of perfect action.

11. Special Prayers for Aspiration

Throughout all lifetimes, wherever I am born,
May I obtain the seven qualities of birth in a higher realm;
May I meet the Dharma immediately after taking birth,
And have the freedom to practice accordingly.

May I please the venerable Spiritual Masters
And practice Dharma day and night.
By understanding the Dharma, and accomplishing its inmost essence,
May I traverse the ocean of worldly existence in that very life.
Within the world may I expound the highest sacred doctrine,
And never become bored or weary of accomplishing the welfare of the others;
And by my own tremendous, impartial service to others
May all beings attain Buddhahood together.

Colophon

This compilation of the Preliminary Practice Prayers of Dzog-pa Chen-po Long-chen Nying-thig is written by the great Tantric yogi Jig-me Trin-lā Wö-zer, who was trained by the gracious kindness of many holy teachers, including Rig-dzin Jig-me Ling-pa, and who achieved confidence in the Law of Tantra. By this merit, may followers see the Guru as the Buddha. Thereby may the self-face of self-awareness, Kun-tu Zang-po, become apparent to them, so that they become the cause of ceaseless benefits for sentient beings endless as the ocean.

Part - II

The Summary of Practice

(A Commentary to the Long-chen Nying-thig Ngon-dro)

-1-

The Common Preliminary Practice

1. The Necessity for Dharma

All sentient beings are alike in their desire for happiness and they wish to avoid experiencing the slightest suffering. To bring such universally shared aims about we should amass the causes for happiness and for the non-arising of misery which, respectively, are to accomplish virtuous actions and to discard unvirtuous ones. This, in accordance with the teachings of the sacred Dharma, is the unexcelled source of benefit and happiness in this as well as all successive lifetimes.

The mundane benefits that accrue from practicing Dharma are such that one will not have to endure servitude to relatives, or defeating enemies because of desire for the status of the former and anger of aggression towards the latter. Nor will one have the hardship of acquiring wealth which one does not have, or of expanding and protecting what one does have. One's mind will be in peace, alert and content, and one will feel affection for and be in harmony with everyone. When the mind is happy, such is its power that even physical illness and misfortunes in general will be surmounted.

The extraordinary benefits that arise out of the pure and complete practice of Dharma are such that one will understand that all elements of cyclic existence are without essence like bubbles; that they are unreal, like an illusion; one's mind will not be disturbed by emotional defilements such as anger and passion; and one will attain realizations and qualities associated with progression through the various spiritual stages and paths, ultimately attaining the state of perfect awakening, Saṃyaksaṃbuddha.

2. The Necessity for the Preliminary Practices

Ordinary beings under the sway of ignorance, unceasingly from beginningless cyclic existence, have believed the elements of the world to be purity, happiness, permanence and selfhood (self-identifiable). Because of this, actions (las; Karma) involving the causes of suffering have been accumulated. Certain aspects of cyclic existence have been held onto as good and we have become attached to them. Other elements have been grasped as bad and aversion to them has developed. Therefore we now experience various sorrows—elements of the Truth of Suffering—in higher and lower states of cyclic existence like a bee trapped in a jar.

Thus since time immemorial has this mind been dwelling (stabilized) in attachment to unholy elements (material elements), grasping them as being real. To practice a spiritual path for merely a short while will not result in much difference to our basic condition other than to accumulate some merit. It would be just like a few drops of water sprinkled upon a forest fire. For a spiritual path to be effective we should practice constantly and progressively utilizing all parts of the mind, bringing into play various skillful means that encompass all aspects of life vigorously and over extended periods of time.

When we apply ourselves specifically to the spiritual development of Buddhadharma, were we to engage in the higher stages of practice directly without the preparation of the common preliminaries, there is a serious danger of deviating onto a wrong path. It would be like giving rich, heavy food to a jaundiced person. To avoid this pitfall one should initially meditate on the foundational practices such as contemplating the "Difficult to obtain fortunate human birth", "The impermanence of life", and so forth. With the significance of these well understood one should proceed through the successive meditations stage by stage.

There are many teachings and texts explaining the various ways for entering the Dharma, ways of training the mind, ways of cultivating oneself in the "view, meditation and practice" and ways of attaining the various "spiritual paths, stages and results". This liturgy, in particular, of the Preliminary Practices of the Long-chen Nying-thig, known as The Excellent Path to Omniscience, the essential teachings from the lineage of Long-chen Rab-jam-pa and Jig-me Ling-pa, although brief, include all the significant points of the path. Although profound in their implication they are easy to practice for those who have faith and the opportunity. In order that these invaluable teachings may be more accessible for practice I have written a summary of this text. Should you experience in your heart the significance of the common preliminary practices, you will be certain that the mundane happiness of the world has no essential reality, and your mind will turn away from attraction toward the limited happiness of cyclic existence. There will be no way then that one would not put the Dharma naturally into practice.

When these preliminary practices have not been assimilated adequately, disturbances such as laziness and erratic wavering in the practice, or disturbances such as attachment to objects of desire or aversion to those which are undesirable arise. If one were to think that contemplations such as "the impermanence of life" are obviously understood, and that there is no need to meditate on them, not only does one cut oneself off from the potential for practicing higher meditations, but does not even possess the qualifications for following the preliminary practices in general. When the mind is prepared through the preliminary practices, just as food is made edible by being cooked, the mind will be capable of entering the actual path of meditation. There will be no likelihood of disturbances such as laziness and fluctuation in the practice, and the meditations will be accomplished.

For the individual whose mind has become involved in the practice of Dharma, the bodily and verbal actions will automatically become wholesome, just as it is said that a tree with medicinal roots will produce leaves and fruit that are medicinal. Similarly it is important that the actions of the body and speech be virtuous. Just as a lamp-glass protects the flame from the wind, the mind will be protected from unskillful actions and lack of inner peace through the appropriately skillful verbal and bodily activities. Thus, if all activities of the three doors of body, speech and mind become virtuous, these actions will accumulate, either directly or indirectly, the two types of goodness or merit—mental and physical. The ultimate culmination of this development will be the understanding of the implication of Reality and Thusness (Chos-nyid-de-bzhin-nyid: dharmatā tathatā) thereby attaining the fully awakened state of being, the state of Buddhahood.

3. The Actual Preliminary Practices

In order to apply oneself to the path to Enlightenment one should train the mind first through the common preliminary practices, and then through the uncommon or extraordinary preliminary practices. The ordinary or extraordinary preliminary practices involve six basic meditations. These are as follows: 1) the difficulty of obtaining a human life with conditions conducive to the practice;

2) even if this is obtained, life is impermanent and there is no likelihood that you will remain alive to complete the practice; 3) death is not the end, one's consciousness transmigrates into rebirth after rebirth, following the karmic actions of virtue and non-virtue; 4) cyclic existence does not lead one beyond suffering, to a state of Nirvāṇa; 5) the attainment of liberation from cyclic existence will establish one in a state of permanent happiness; 6) to attain such liberation one should follow a qualified master who is capable of faultlessly guiding one along the spiritual path.

With an understanding of the meaning of these six interrelated topics one should begin the recitation of the practice from "the rare privilege of a perfect human rebirth" (da.res.dmyal.ba. etc.), the common preliminary prayer.

i. The rare privilege of a human rebirth

It is exceedingly important to recognize the opportunity afforded by obtaining a human life endowed with the 18 conditions favorable for the practice of Dharma. There are said to be eight states of confinement of hell beings, hungry spirits, animals, long-lived gods, barbarians, heretics, in a land devoid of Buddhist teaching, or to have been born as a deaf-mute. Freedom from such confinement or limitation of spiritual development is said to encompass freedom (dal.ba) from these eight states. However, we also require birth not just as a human being, but in a life where we have ten favorable endowments ('byor.ba). These are to have been born as a human in a land open to the practice of Dharma, to have all one's senses functioning, to avoid wrong actions and to have faith in the Buddha's teachings, these being internal endowments. The five remaining endowments that are externally required are to have been born when a fully awakened being has come, when he has taught, when the teachings are flourishing, when there are realized followers and when one has direct contact with a Spiritual Master. To possess these 18 freedoms and endowments comprises the "precious human birth".

The difficulty of obtaining this rare privilege is evident from examining its causes, citing examples and considering its rarity from a numerical standpoint.

From the point of view of its causes this precious human life is rare because the basis for its attainment lies in pure ethical discipline, together with the support of skillful actions such as generosity. For these causes to be linked to the appropriate result, namely the precious human rebirth, the pure aspiration for this to take place must also be present. Yet there are few people who, within this present life, act in such a way that these favorable circumstances will continue tin the future life.

As an example of the rarity of a precious human birth the Buddha said, "Consider a yoke floating about the vastness of the ocean, and a blind turtle who surfaces only once in every hundred years. It is easier for the turtle to poke his head through the yoke than for someone to obtain a precious human birth."

Numerically, the Buddha has said that the number of sentient beings in hell is equal to the number of atoms in the earth, and in the realms of gods and men the number of beings is equal to the number of atoms between the white and dark portions of a fingernail. Then he said that generally, among human beings, those who practice Dharma properly are less than stars in the daytime.

To have contemplated these points seriously will make us realize that it is exceedingly rare and difficult to obtain this precious human rebirth. This being so, we should feel privileged to have obtained this opportunity and should determine to make this life meaningful by cultivating spiritual values. For instance, to obtain by meditative state of one pointedness, one must practice diligently and develop various attainments. From the energy for such a concerted effort can arise part of the realization of this perfect human birth. One of the Ka-dam-pa Geshes, Chan-nga-wa (spyan.snga.ba), practiced only his meditation; he never slept. Geshe Ton-pa (ston.pa) told him "Son, you have to take some rest, otherwise you will be in danger of getting sick." Geshe chan-nga-wa replied, "It is true what you say, but I have no time to rest because I am thinking about the difficulty of obtaining this fortunate human life."

The great Indian pandit Shantideva, in his Guide to the Boddhisattva's Way of Life (Byang.chub.sems.dpa'i.spyod-pa.la. 'jug.pa: Bodhisattvacharyāvatāra) Chapt. I, stanza 4, says:

> These leisures and endowments are very hard to obtain;
> And, when one has the chance to fulfill the aim of humanity.
> And fails to take advantage now,
> How will such a perfect opportunity arise again?

ii. The impermanence of life

It is foolhardy to delay in applying oneself seriously to the practice, now that this opportunity has been obtained, by first finishing off one's worldly obligations. There will never be a time when worldly activities will be completed. Their flow is like the waves of an ocean following one upon another. The nature of life is changing from moment to moment, and ever-present are unknown causes which may lead to death, like a candle flame in a strong wind. This being so, one must determine to practice the Dharma from this moment on.

Impermanence is the nature of all conditioned phenomena. Mountains, forests and all sentient beings from the highest, wisest saints, scientists and realized beings, down to itinerant beggars and the smallest insect—anything that can be thought of are all identical in their impermanence, for they change and disintegrate from moment to moment. With every breath we race toward death, the target for the arrow of our life. We do not know when we will die, or under what circumstances death will occur. If we simply exhaled and failed to inhale we would die. So the distance between life and death is the space between one breath and the next.

Death may be caused by an imbalance of any of the physical bodily elements, or may be caused by external factors such as natural calamities, poison, weapons and so forth. It is difficult to anticipate whether one will be alive tomorrow or not. If we ponder on the imminence of death repeatedly, arriving at some understanding of it, then the obstructions to practice such as laziness, attachment to pleasure, and procrastination will automatically be dispelled, and one will not remain without practicing from this moment on, just as one would not remain comfortable if one's head were on fire. Until this point is reached we must extend our practice.

One example of the developed awareness of impermanence is the Geshe Kha-rag Gom-chung (kha.rag.sgom.chung), who was meditating in a cave at Kha-rag hermitage in Tsang, a province of central Tibet. Outside the entrance to his cave was a thorn bush, so close to his passage that when he entered his clothing was torn. He had thought of cutting down the bush, but then, reflected, "Perhaps I shall die before I come out. it is better to spend the time on practice instead of cutting down the bush." Then when he came out he thought, "I may die before going in again, so it is better to spend the time in practice." He spent many years meditating and attained high accomplishments (dngos.sgrub; siddhi), but never cut down the bush because of this intense awareness of impermanence.

Buddha Shakyamuni has stated in the Lalitavistara Sūtra:

> The three worlds are as impermanent as clouds in the autumn sky;
> Beings' births and deaths are like watching a dance;
> The duration of people's lives is like a flash of lightning;
> It passes as swiftly as a stream down a steep mountain.

iii. Karma: the cause and result of action

The Indian teacher Vasubandhu, in his text called The Treasury of Phenomenology (chos.mngon.mdzod; Abhidharmakoṣha), says:

> From karmic actions the various states of cyclic existence arise.

All the variations within the world, and all the various states of cyclic existence, appear due to the different kinds of actions of Karma committed by beings. These states of existence are unceasing in their continuation, and in fact are a product of actions that living beings have committed in lifetimes before. One does not simply disappear after death, but the mind, which is non-physical by nature, continues beyond the body, taking birth again according to the weight of specific actions performed during that lifetime. The particulars of the life in which we find ourselves and in which we observe other beings, are not randomly caused but are the result of specific virtuous or non-virtuous actions we have previously committed. One experiences happiness as a result of skillful actions, and suffering as a result of wrongdoing. Although all sentient beings desire happiness and do not want to suffer, they neither have the opportunity, such as is afforded by the human birth, to accumulate virtue nor to abandon wrong actions. Accordingly, they are sinking in the ocean of suffering of cyclic existence. We, however, as human beings, have the intelligence to recognize virtuous and non-virtuous actions and are capable of practicing the acceptance of wholesome actions and the rejection of unwholesome actions faultlessly. To realize this is important.

Complete understanding of the process of karmic actions is extremely difficult. Fully awakened beings, and the great meditators of the past, who possess omniscient wisdom, have direct perception of their existence. Even on a more usual level there are numerous instances reported of small children who remember their previous lives, and recognize their possessions from a preceding existence. There are cases of ghosts of the departed entering living bodies and speaking through a medium. We should not totally disregard these occurrences, but should view them as instances that prove the existence of the mind outside the realm of the body. In this way we may come to know of the existence of reincarnation. On the mind are placed latencies from the actions we have done, and these determine the extent to which we find ourselves in either happiness or misery, either in this or in future lifetimes. Virtuous and non-virtuous actions are many, although in brief we can classify ten non-virtuous actions of the body, speech and mind which arise from the poisonous defilements of anger, desire or ignorance.

There are three wholesome actions of the body: refraining from destroying life, or making an effort to save others' lives; refraining from taking the possessions of others without their being given, or practicing generosity; refraining from wrong conduct in sexual desires, or keeping oneself morally pure. There are four skillful actions of speech: refraining from false speech, or speaking the truth; refraining from slander, or reconciling enemies; refraining from harsh speech, or speaking harmoniously; and refraining from foolish chatter, or reciting prayers. There are three virtuous actions of the mind: refraining from covetousness, or being generous; refraining from malice, or arousing benevolence; and refraining from holding wrong views, or developing the correct understanding of reality.

If one has a natural belief in the process of karmic actions, one will act spontaneously according to the principles governing the way it functions. One will not have the heart to take the life of even an insect, nor for telling a single lie. Since such as awareness can only lead to increased happiness and contentment, it is important to be alert in one's actions with full faith in the principles of their process. Milarepa, one of Tibet's greatest practitioners, poets and saints, had acute understanding of the process of Karma. Early in his life he committed very great non-virtue in bringing about the death of a large number of relatives and friends, but later, out of his understanding of the process of Karma, he felt a great regret for these previous actions and practiced the Dharma from his heart, purifying all traces of these actions and later attaining complete realization of the Path.

The Buddha, in the Rājāvavādaka Sūtra, has said:

> If, when his time comes, even a king should die,
> His wealth, friends and relatives shall not follow him.

Wherever men go, wherever they remain,
Their actions, like a shadow, will follow them.

iv. The suffering of saṃsāra

From beginningless time sentient beings have been wandering ceaselessly through the higher and lower states of the six realms of rebirth within cyclic existence. This is all in accordance with their actions, or Karma. Even in the case of a powerful man who in this life has the finest enjoyments the world can give, it is not certain that within cyclic existence he would not become, after death, fuel for the fires of hell. That which determines this is not the specific form of the life at present but the actions that we engage in during this life. Realms of hellish states or existence of great happiness are a product of the workings of Karma. And yet even these variations within cyclic existence are still in the nature of suffering.

Generally, no matter where we may be reborn, there is no place where we will not be afflicted by one of the three major forms of suffering: that of suffering in general—birth, old age, sickness and death; that of change—the transitory nature of phenomena and states of pain and pleasure; and that suffering which is pervasive with simply being born within one of the six realms of cyclic existence.

There are said to be six realms of suffering within cyclic existence, which, in brief, may be understood as follows: where one has a preponderance of anger, this will lead to rebirth in a hell realm where one will experience the suffering of intense heat and cold for great periods of time; if one has a preponderance of avarice or greed, one will be reborn as a hungry spirit, and will experience the misery of unsatiated thirst and hunger; as a result of ignorance and stupidity one will experience the misery of dumb animals, and will be forced to labor for others or would be afraid of being eaten by other beings; to be excessively jealous will lead to suffering in the realm of the demi-gods, where one will have to endure being engaged in fighting; as a result of desire one will have to undergo the suffering of the human state, involving birth, illness, ageing and death; and the outcome of pride is such that one will take birth among celestial beings where one will experience the suffering of dying and falling into lower realms of rebirth. If we take ourselves as an example we will observe that we are always experiencing the various kinds of human suffering, such as birth, ageing, illness and death, and we also suffer from the apprehension of encountering enemies or losing friends. We also suffer from not obtaining what brings us pleasure and from receiving unwanted problems.

If we extend our contemplation and reflect again and again that there is nothing but suffering in the world, we will achieve detachment from cyclic existence and will desire nothing but liberation from its confines. Just as if we place a bowl of fried food before a jaundiced person. Until we have a similar feeling for the ephemeral pleasures of the world we should continue to cultivate understanding of the basic dissatisfactory nature of cyclic existence. One instance of the awareness of the suffering of the world was the Geshe Lang-ri Thang-pa (glang.ri.thang.pa), whose companion told him that other Lamas were calling him "The grim-faced Lang-ri Thang-pa". He replied, "While thinking about the sufferings of cyclic existence, how can one look cheerful?"

Buddha Shakyamuni has stated:

> Due to desire, becoming and ignorance,
> Beings will revolve foolishly through the five realms—
> Those of humans, gods and the three inferior realms—
> Like the turning of a potter's wheel.

v. The benefits of liberation

Total freedom from all states of cyclic existence that are included in two of the four noble truths, that of suffering and that of the origin of suffering, is termed liberation. This is also known as the state beyond sorrow, or Nirvāṇa, a state which is beyond the limitations imposed by the ignorant mind that is unaware of the basic nature of reality, and that perpetrates the sufferings of the world. In general there are numerous common and extraordinary qualities that are the outcome of such an attainment. These may vary in accordance with the variety of approaches to the spiritual paths and results, namely those approaches of the Disciples or the Hearers (nyan.thos; shrāvakas), Self-realized Ones (rang.rgyal; Pratyekabuddha), the Awakening Warriors (byang.chub.sems.dpa'; Bodhisattva) or the Tantric Practitioner.

The goal attained by all these means, that are appropriate to the various dispositions of people, is perpetual liberation (thar.pa; mokṣha) from the ocean of cyclic existence. This results in the possession of the citadel of Enlightenment in the city of peace and bliss. One should be aware that this is the goal to be realized and these are its attributes.

vi. The value of a spiritual guide

The spiritual path to the attainment of liberation is both extensive and profound, and involves the progressive attainment of spiritual insight. The most important prerequisite is to have a competent Spiritual Master to guide one, a teacher who exhibits the necessary qualifications, in the same way that when we wish to cross an ocean we must have an experienced pilot.

Once such a teacher has been encountered one should act according to his instructions, just as one would heed those of a doctor in order to cure an illness. On the other hand, spiritual arrogance, where one thinks one can practice meditation without any guidance, gives one little chance not to deviate along a wrong path.

It is also important to precisely examine whether or not your teacher is qualified, otherwise you may not receive any benefits. There is a danger, in following one who is incompetent, of being seriously misled. It would be like a falling man who clutches out to another falling man for his help. Moreover, from a spiritual point of view, serious obstacles are created if we have a teacher whom we later find to be unqualified and then lose faith in him. Thus it is very important to examine the spiritual qualities of the person before taking him as one's own teacher. After one has found a proficient master one should receive teachings from him which ripen and purify the mind. One must do as he instructs without any doubt or hesitation, with great respect and strong belief that all he says involves the pure teaching, and all he does is an expression of excellence.

-2-

The Uncommon Preliminary Practice

Once our mind has been trained and acquainted with the principles set out in the common Preliminary Practices, and we experience a natural, unmodified and spontaneous desire to practice Dharma, we are fully ready to enter the door of spiritual practice. To do so, specifically in relation to Mahayana Buddhism, it is necessary to embark on those Preliminary Practices not common to all spiritual traditions. These involve specifically Buddhist oriented practices, such as Taking Refuge, and include the following topics:

1. Taking refuge in the Three Supreme Jewels (dkon.mchog.gsum.: Tri Ratna), namely the guide or teacher, the spiritual path or his teaching, and the companions along the way to the state of liberation. Refuge is the foundation stone of all Dharma practice.
2. Activating the Awakening Mind (byang.chub.kyi.sems.; Bodhicitta), the entrance into and the very heart of the Great Vehicle (theg.pa.chen.po.; Mahāyāna).
3. Reciting the mantra of an meditating upon the form of Vajrasattva (rdo.rje.sems.pa) in order to purify one's emotional defilements, the obstructions against the attainment of liberation from the process of cyclic existence.
4. Offering the maṇḍala or universe to the Lama, the ultimate spiritual principal. This is for the accumulation of merit (bsod.nams.; puṇya) or stock of positive energy which brings together causes favorable to the attainment of realization.
5. Making prostrations which purify emotional defilements as well as accumulate merit.

It is considered essential within the lineage of this specific teaching to have completed one hundred thousand repetitions of each of these five practices. This is done to prepare the mind for the higher meditations directly relevant to the Dzog-chen meditation. Traditionally, if one has not done so, one is neither permitted to receive a teaching nor even to read a page of scripture relating to the higher practices.

1. Going for Refuge

Going for refuge in the Three Supreme Jewels and observing the attendant obligations is said to be like the door to Dharma. And individual, properly speaking, may not consider him or herself a Buddhist without having sincerely gone for refuge. Refuge may be the entrance into the Dharma, but the key to unlocking this door is faith. It is impossible to seek refuge in something in which one lacks any faith; thus it is first essential to learn and appreciate the qualities of the Three Supreme Jewels. Such an appreciation will lead to the development of the three aspects of faith, namely: cleansing faith, which is a natural responsiveness to manifestations of the Dharma with the effect of cleansing the mind; aspirational faith, which is an urge to practice Dharma and to obtain its results; and believing faith, which is based on a conviction of the validity of the teachings. Without faith, not even a single virtue will arise. In the Ratnakuta sutra it is stated, "If a man has no faith, no virtue will arise in him, just as a seed burnt by fire will produce no green shoot."

There are a number of different levels involved in taking refuge. These depend on our own capacity and inclination of mind. First, in accordance with the way common to Buddhism in general, we take refuge by respecting the Buddha as the guide along the path, the Dharma as the spiritual path, and the Sangha as the support in practicing the path.

According to the Vajrayana or Tantric tradition of Buddhism, which is not found in all traditions, there are subtler levels in which we can take refuge. The first of these relates to the first stage of Tantric practice, the developing stage (bskyed.rim.; utpattikrama) in which we take refuge by offering our "three doors"—our body, speech and mind—to the lama as refuge in the Buddha; we devote ourself to the personal deity (yi.dam.; iṣhta-devatā) or inner refuge as the path; and we should view the Ḍāka or Ḍākinī (mkha'.'gro or mkha'-'gro.ma) as the spiritual support on the path. Over and above this form of refuge is that which relates to the completion stage (rdzogs.rim; utpannakrama) of the Highest Yoga Tantra in which we take refuge in the true nature, the Awakening Mind or Bodhicitta (which in the Tantric practice is linked with the unchanging Great Bliss). In this case the Saṇgha refuge means a recognition of the practice's dependence upon the physical channel system (rtsa; nāḍi) which is understood as the perfect body of Emanation (sprul.sku; Nirmāṇakāya); the Dharma refuge is understanding the purification of the physical wind or energy (rlung; vayu) as the perfect body of Complete Enjoyment (longs.sku; Saṃbhogakāya); and the Buddha refuge is realizing the purification of our seminal essence (thig.le; bindu) to be the perfect body of Truth (chos.sku; Dharmakāya).

The highest and most subtle form of Refuge is that which is known as Refuge in the Vajra Nature (gnas. lugs.rdo.rje). This is the determination to realize the three inseparable aspects of Primordial Wisdom (ye.shes; jñāna) present in the mind of the refuge objects; its Empty Essence as the Dharmakāya, the Buddha Refuge; its Lucid Nature as the Saṃbhogakāya, the Dharma Refuge; and its Universal Compassion as the Nirmāṇakāya, the Saṇgha Refuge. The significance of these Tantric ways of taking Refuge will only be fully appreciated as direct experience is gained in the practices.

There are various attitudes that may be present when we go for refuge. We may take refuge to protect us from the suffering of lower realms of existence and to ensure that we are reborn in the happy states of existence. Such is the motive of an inferior person. If we take refuge for the liberation of ourselves from Saṃsāra our motivation is that of an individual of middling capacity. To take refuge with the wish to lead all sentient beings to the final attainment of Buddhahood is to do so with the supreme motivation of the superior person. Within this context we are concerned with taking refuge as a person of superior motivation.

When taking refuge we must receive it directly from a qualified teacher and follow the obligations connected with it. Once refuge has been taken directly from a Spiritual Master it is possible to follow the practice through a form such as in this prayer. We should be seated comfortably, preferably in a meditation posture, and should visualize in our mind's eye the Assembly Tree (tshogs.zhing) which is the object before which we accumulate merit. Holding this visualization before us we should recite the refuge stanza commencing, "To the actual Three Rare and Supreme Jewels...". We should take refuge with the thought that "until all beings attain Enlightenment I shall go for refuge in these Three Rare and Supreme Jewels." This should be recited with strong conviction and reverence, and with one-pointedness of mind. After repeating this three times, one should imagine that all sentient beings, including oneself, dissolve into the Assembly Tree, that all the objects within the Assembly Tree dissolve into the central figure of the Spiritual Master, and that he in turn dissolves into "utter simplicity" (spros.bral), the absolute inactivity of Thusness, and one should continue in the truly natural meditative state of Refuge for as long as possible.

In brief, the obligations of taking Refuge are never to seek protection in any worldly gods or material goals, this being counter to the refuge in Buddha; never to harm sentient beings, which is counter to the Truth of Dharma; and never to associate with people of perverted views and behavior, this being counter to refuge in the Sangha.

According to the higher Tantric practices we should consider, with devotion and without any doubt, that all the objects of refuge are present in the nature of the Spiritual Master. His mind is the Buddha, his speech is the Dharma and his body is the Sangha.

Generally, to have faith in anything will bring benefits accordingly. The benefits obtained by the practitioner do not depend on the excellence or lack of it of the objects of faith, but only upon the individual's mind and quality of faith. Thus it is very important to have what is known as the attitude which views all appearances as pure (dag.snang). This we can understand from Tibetan stories such as those of the old woman khyi-so sang-gya, who attained Liberation through her devout veneration of a dog's tooth, and those stories of Kongpo Ben (rkong.po.'ben). Therefore the great teacher Padmasambhava has said, "One shall receive blessings by having faith, and will obtain all that is desired if there are no doubts in the mind."

2. Activating the Awakening Mind

In order to realize the principles embodied in the Three Jewels by means of seeking Refuge in the causes for such a state, which are themselves also the Three Jewels, one must practice virtuous actions. These actions of the Bodhisattva are diverse and varied. However, to engage in these activities, it is first necessary to develop bodhicitta, the thought of enlightenment, the Awakening Mind. Cultivation of the Awakening Mind is the way of the Great Vehicle, the Mahāyāna. It is the entrance into the Mahāyāna as well as the very heart of it.

Bodhicitta is the thought of freeing all sentient beings from suffering and the causes of suffering, and of leading them to dwell in bliss and happiness until they are completely freed, and finally to establish them in the realm of supreme enlightenment, the fully awakened state of being. To do so we should seize this highest of thoughts by feeling, "I shall act for the perfect benefit of all others by attaining supreme enlightenment myself and by practicing the innumerable activities of the Bodhisattvas, such as the Transcending Perfections (pha.rol.tu.phyin.pa; Pāramitā) and so on." If such a thought arises within us, from that moment onwards we shall be known as a Bodhisattva, or a son of the Conqueror, and will be venerated by gods and men. Whether working or resting our spiritual merit continuously will increase like the unrestricted growth of saplings.

It is said that by accumulating such merit over three measureless aeons, one will perfect the Five Spiritual Paths and Ten Spiritual Stages and will attain Buddhahood, their result. We may think that since this is a tremendously long period of time there is nothing extraordinary about such a spiritual path. To think so is wrong. By cultivating an especially strong and pure thought to benefit others in an ultimate way, it is possible to complete the accumulation of merit rapidly. This is born out in one of the former life-stories of the Buddha, when he was known as the ship's pilot Nying-je-chen. He realized one of the passengers of the ship, a black man known as Dung-thung-chen, was about to kill all on board and to plunder the ship's cargo. With immense compassion, both for him and for his potential victims, Nying-je-chen took the life of this man, and in one instant of this great compassion perfected the merit of seventy thousand aeons. You may also think that it is inappropriate to attain liberation from cyclic existence for ourselves since we have vowed to act for the benefit of others until all beings have attained the realm of enlightenment. Such an assumption is not correct. If we attain Nirvāṇa, or the state "Beyond Sorrow", our activities on behalf of others will not cease. Even though it is stated that the fully awakened mind has no conceptual intention to benefit others and acts with total spontaneity, due to the interdependence (rten.'brel; pratītyasamutpāda) of the aspirations and wishes cultivated during the period of practice (slob.lam;shaikṣhamārga), until all sentient beings attain full realization our activities for the welfare of others will appear spontaneously within cyclic existence.

To cultivate the Awakening Mind we can prepare by means of the Four Boundless Practices. First we should understand that it is never certain who are friends or enemies, and whether they always stay that way. Developing an unbiased attitude without hatred towards enemies or attachment towards friends is the state of "boundless equanimity". Secondly, there is no sentient being who, in innumerable previous lifetimes, has never been our parent. To wish that they should have happiness is known as "boundless love". "Boundless compassion" is the wish to see all sentient beings separated from suffering. And to find happiness in the happiness and joy of others is the cultivation of "boundless joy".

One should accept the precepts of a Bodhisattva from a qualified Lama, one who has the attributes of a Mahāyāna teacher. One should, through offerings, amass as large an accumulation of merit as possible. After completing the actual ceremony one should observe the precepts related to it. In this practice we do so by reciting the stanza beginning, "Deceived by myriad appearances...". Again in this instance the Assembly Tree is visualized in the sky above us, and we should activate the Awakening Mind by reflecting, with gratitude, upon the sufferings of all sentient beings who have, at one time or another, been our mothers. Together with this we should have the absolute determination to lead them out of their suffering and unto the state of supreme enlightenment. These thoughts should pervade our mind during this practice, and at the end of the meditation period, as the divinities of the Assembly Tree dissolve into us, we should think that the ultimate Awakening Mind embodied in the Assembly Tree is activated within. This ultimate Awakening Mind is emptiness (stong.pa.nyid; Shūnyatā) and our mind should remain stabilized in it.

Generally, although there are many ways of dividing Bodhicitta, if we look at it according to the degree of mental power we have three main divisions, each of which reflect a successively lesser aspiration. First, the King-like development of Bodhicitta involves the thought that one will attain Enlightenment first and afterwards will lead all sentient beings to that state. The Boatman-like development of Bodhicitta is the desire for one's own Enlightenment and that of others together. The Shepherd-like development of Bodhicitta is the urge to lead all sentient beings to Buddhahood first and then to attain it oneself. We should practice according to our own inclination and capacity.

Aside from this there are various aspects of the practices relating to the cultivation of Bodhicitta which may take place over three immeasurable aeons. The most generally accepted division of the practice itself is in terms of the intentional Bodhicitta, which is like the wish to go somewhere, and the actual Bodhicitta, which is like the journey itself. The former involves the thought that I shall lead all sentient beings to Buddhahood, and is practiced through three different meditations. There is meditation on the equality of self and others and understanding that our aspirations for happiness and the avoidance of suffering are no different than the aspirations of all other beings; meditation on the exchange of oneself with others in which we transfer the normal egocentric attitude we have towards ourself and our aims and aspirations onto the aims and aspirations of others, and in which the usual disregard we have for others is now focused upon ourself; and meditation in which we care for others more than ourself. These are all meditations fundamentally centered around the aspirational Bodhicitta.

To train in cultivating the actual Awakening Mind, which is like actually venturing into the journey itself, involves many different aspects. However, they may be summarized in the Six Transcending Perfections, the Paramitas. These we must practice.

First is the Transcending Perfection of Giving, or Generosity (sbyin.pa; dāna). This involves giving, without any attachment, worldly possessions and material objects, religious or spiritual instructions and teachings, and giving protection from fear in an ultimate sense. The Perfection of Moral Discipline (tsul.khrims.; shīla) also has three aspects. We should abandon non-virtuous action, we should accumulate and practice following virtuous actions, and we should act for the sake of other beings by means of the four ways of gathering disciples. These four ways of gathering disciples are to be generous, to be gentle in speech, to behave according to the principles of Dharma and to act for the welfare of others. The Transcending Perfection of Patience (bzod.pa;kṣhānti) involves three main practices. To return anger or abuse or injury with love and action for the benefit of the harmer is known as the "patience in which the opposite is done"; forbearance over thirst and hunger for the sake of spiritual practice is called the "patience or endurance of difficulties for Dharma"; to have no fear upon hearing the profound meaning of subjects such as Emptiness, and allow ourselves time to comprehend their meaning, is called the "patience of fearlessness over the profound meaning". The Transcending Perfection of Spiritual Endeavor or Effort (brtson.'grus.; vīrya) involves three aspects. To be diligent without dismay is to wear the "armor of enthusiasm"; to apply ourselves immediately to spiritual practice without falling under the sway of procrastination, is called the "involvement of enthusiasm"; to never be satisfied with doing a little spiritual practice and to always have the desire for more, continuously applying oneself, is called "unsatisfied enthusiasm".

The Perfection of Meditative Stability or Concentration (bsam.brtan.; dhyāna) should be done in a solitary place without distraction or internal hindrances such as laziness. This again has three aspects. To have attachment to imaginary projections of bliss (bde.ba), clarity (gsal.ba), and freedom from conceptions (mi.rtog.pa) and to meditate with attachment on such imaginary projections is called the "small boy's concentration". To be detached from these imaginary projections and yet to experience no taste of the meditation, and to meditate with attachment to the "antidote", grasping it as "Emptiness", is called the concentration which "analyzes the (profound) meaning". To be detached from this notion of the antidote, namely the grasping of emptiness, and to remain in a state of concentration on reality itself without any conceptual thoughts, is called the "Tathāgata concentration". The first two of these aspects of concentration involve distractions from the heart of the practice.

The Transcending Perfection of Wisdom or Discriminating Intelligence (shes.rab.; prajñā) can also involve three points. The intelligence of "hearing" is to understand the meaning of the words spoken by the Spiritual Master. The intelligence of "contemplating" is to ponder and consider deeply the meaning of what has been heard. After clearing away doubts by hearing and contemplating, it is necessary to meditate on the meaning. One will come to understand that all appearing objects are delusory or deceptive in nature. This will arise through observing that the five objects of sensory perception, objects of taste, touch, smell, sight and hearing, are ultimately without any essence, like the eight examples of Māyā. Once this is understood one should examine the nature of the subject, namely the mind to which these things are appearing. In this case the appearance of the object will not cease, but the thought grasping at the object as real will be terminated. In such a way one will come to understand the meditation in which reality itself is like the sky (chos.nyid.nam.mkha'.lta.bu). This is known as the intelligence or wisdom of "meditation". These three wisdoms, that of hearing, contemplation and meditation are the backbone of a thorough practice.

3. Meditation and Recitation of Vajrasattva

Tendencies towards unskillful actions and emotional defilements obstruct the mind which seeks to understand the meaning of the practice and to follow deep meditation. To enable the reflection of unders tanding and knowledge to arise in "the mirror of the universal ground", it is very important to cleanse this mirror through purification. Emotional obstructions can be purified through many ways, yet the most efficacious way is through the practice of confession by means of the Vajrasattva Practice incorporating four effective antidotes.

Generally there is nothing good in non-virtuous action, but if it is confessed non-virtue will be purified. This is its only redeeming good quality. It is impossible, if confession is done with the four opponent forces, that the non-virtuous action will not be purified. The first of these opponent forces is the force of "reliance". This means looking upon the visualized image of Vajrasattva as the embodiment of one's Refuge. The second opponent force is the force of "sincere regret". Non-virtuous actions can never be purified without a feeling of remorse or regret at having committed them. Thus we should reveal these wrong actions without holding back any feeling, as though these actions are poisons that have entered one's body and need to be eliminated. The force of "abandoning negative actions" is the thought to never commit such an action again in the future, even were it to cost us our life. The fourth opponent force, that of "applying counter-measures", is to engage in practices which purify the mind and accumulate merit, directing their power expressly against unskillful wrong actions and, especially in this case, practicing the meditation and recitation of Vajrasattva without parting from aspiration of the Awakening Mind while remaining in the unmodified state of reality.

i. The Visualization

In the space above the crown of one's head visualize at the center of a thousand-petalled lotus, standing on a full moon, a white letter HŪṂ. This instantly becomes the nature of one's principal teacher, the total embodiment of all Fully Awakened Beings, appearing in the form of Vajrasattva (Dor-je Sem-pa) who is in fact a divine manifestation of all the wisdom, compassion and power of the Awakened Beings, specifically for the purification of wrongdoings and emotional defilements.

We should imagine his body as white like a snow-mountain reflecting the light of one hundred thousand suns. He has one face and two hands, his right hand holding at his heart a five-pronged vajra scepter indicating the empty nature of pure awareness (rig.stong). His left hand rests on his left hip and holds the bell symbolic of the union of empty nature and appearance (snang.stong). His two legs are crossed in the Vajra-posture. He is adorned with the 13 costumes associated with the perfect body of Complete Enjoyment, the Saṃbhogakāya. These are comprised of the five costumes of silk, namely head-scarf, shoulder covering, a silk stole, a belt and a lower skirt-like garment, together with the eight precious ornaments the crown, earrings, necklace, armlets, long and short chest pendants, bracelets, finger rings and anklets.

He is in union with his consort Vajrabhṛikuṭī who is holding in her right hand a curved vajra-blade and in her left a skull brimming with nectar. In the heart of the united consorts, on a small moon the size of a crushed mustard seed, is a white HŪṂ as if inscribed there by a single hair. This is surrounded by three concentric circles comprised of the one hundred letters of Vajrasattva's mantra, commencing from the front. This visualization should be seen without mixing any other images, clear like a rainbow. It is accomplished by the manifestation of one's own wisdom. We should pray one-pointedly, employing the Five Strengths of Meditation, and begin reciting the hundred-syllable mantra of Vajrasattva. As we do so white nectar with rays of light cascade from the letters in the heart of the consorts and pass down through the point of union. These lights and rays enter into the body of ourself and others through the crown of our head and spread throughout our body. All our bad actions, emotional defilements, wrongdoings, illnesses and so forth are imagined as filth and soot and are forced out of the body through the soles of the feet and the lower orifices, and through the pores of the skin so the body becomes purified, in the form of light filled with bliss which is empty by nature.

At the completion of the practice Vajrasattva inspires one by saying, "Your wrongdoings and defilements are hereby purified". Vajrasattva himself spontaneously melts into light rays which then dissolve into oneself so that one becomes transformed into Vajrasattva oneself. Now in the heart of oneself as Vajrasattva, on a moon, visualize a blue HŪṂ. In front of it is white OṂ, at the right a yellow VAJRA, at the back a red SA and on the left a green TVA as if written by a hair. We should concentrate on them and recite the short form of the mantra, OṂ VAJRASATTVA HŪṂ. Light rays are emitted from the letters, and these going out and touching the Fully Awakened Beings in the numerous Pure Realms, offerings of the great wisdom of Bliss and Emptiness are made. This satisfies the Buddhas and one's own accumulation of merit is accomplished.

All their blessings are drawn back in the form of rays and dissolve into the letters, achieving the common and uncommon attainments (dngos.sgrub.; siddhi).

Again we should imagine that these rays of light are emitted from our heart, and this time when they come in contact with the Enlightened Beings in the Pure Realms, they emit the sound of the mantra. At the very end of the meditation we should imagine that all visualized objects dissolve into ourself and we in turn dissolve into the mantra at our heart, and that also dissolves letter by letter into the HŪṂ in its center. This HŪṂ slowly dissolves upwards and finally disappears into the dot above it. This dot also eventually disappears like a rainbow and at the end of the meditative period we should remain in a state of non-conceptualization of the three previously mentioned meditative factors. This is the ultimate purification of all emotional and karmic defilements.

After rising from that meditation session, while engaged in ordinary activities, we should also reflect that the world and all beings in it are like a divine container and its contents, and thereby take every aspect of daily life into the path of practice.

4. Maṇḍala Offering

According to this text there are two practices related to offering of the maṇḍala which accumulate merit. The main one is the Maṇḍala Offering proper and the secondary practice is known as the Mendicant's Accumulation of Merit (ku.su.lu'i.tshogs.bsag) The purpose of the preceding practice was to dispel unfavorable obstructions by purification of non-virtuous deeds. This alone is insufficient for realization to be attained. One should additionally accumulate merit in order to build up more and more favorable conditions for experiencing the essence of the path. Without the accumulation of merit one will never attain complete realization nor will one understand the meaning of Emptiness. Thus it is essential to cultivate the dual accumulation of both physical merit and mental wisdom. On this method, Tilopa has said, "O Naropa, my son: until you have understood that the appearance of interdependence relationships is not produced, do not depart from the two wheels of the chariot of accumulation of merit and wisdom." A tantra also states, "Without the accumulation of merit there will be no result, just as oil cannot be extracted from sand."

Fundamentally the maṇḍala practice is an offering both of materials and of mentally visualized objects, of all the finest things both within and without cyclic existence, to the most excellent of objects, the Three Supreme Jewels. Since innumerable forms of accumulation of merit are included in the Maṇḍala practice, it is one of the best ways to accomplish the path. First in the actual practice we should amass the finest materials that we can as our material objects of offering. These should be arrayed on an altar or suitable place. Next we should visualize the Assembly Tree, the object of our offering, as when we go for Refuge. The accumulation of merit in this practice is accomplished primarily by means of offering through mental visualization. Although there are many methods of offering the Maṇḍala, here we are concerned with the offering to the Three Perfect Bodies or the Three Kāyas.

The Nirmāṇakāya Maṇḍala Offering involves all the beings and the world systems, including oneself and one's possessions, being offered to the assembly of Nirmāṇakāya manifestations. This is known as the common Nirmāṇakāya Maṇḍala Offering. Above this imagined universe we should visualize the Pure Land of Beautifully Arrayed Akanishṭha which has the five certainties associated with the Saṃbhogakāya state, namely the certainty of place, teacher, disciples, doctrine and time. This is an unimaginable array of palaces ornamented by numerous goddesses of offering, and it is they whom we present to the assembly of Saṃbhogakāya forms in the visualized Refuge Tree. This is known as the uncommon Saṃbhogakāya Maṇḍala. Above this is the Dharmakāya Maṇḍala, the highest of all. In this case we build the offering out of all thoughts arising from the manifestation of unceasing luminosity, the fourfold vision and so forth, heaped upon a base of the unborn Dharmadhātu. All this is offered to the assembly of the Dharmakāya. All this is offered to the assembly of the Dharmakāya. Although this visualization is described in terms of 'above' and 'below', "above the Nirmāṇakāya" and so forth, in actuality there is no question of partially of extremes—there is no 'above and below'. With this in mind and with our visualization clear, we should recite the relevant stanzas. We should make nine heaps on the maṇḍala plate for the Nirmāṇakāya, five heaps for the Saṃbhogakāya and one for the Dharmakāya. Conversely we may recite the 37 heap Maṇḍala Offering, or if we are not able to do that we may complete the practice by reciting the shortest form, the seven-heaped Offering.

The second form of Maṇḍala Offering here, the Mendicant's Accumulation of Merit, is a special way practiced by simple yogis.

It is called Chö (gcod) which means "cutting off" or severing the four demonic influences simultaneously. The four demonic forces are (1) Kamadeva, the god of lust, (2) the demon of death, (3) the demon of emotional defilements, and (4) the demon of the aggregates. It is an aspect of the practice for accumulation merit. Generally we are far more attached to our body than to any possessions, so to cut off attachment to our body and to give it away is more beneficial than any other kind of offering. In the practice of Chö the objects to whom the offerings are made are visualized in the sky above us and the offering objects themselves are imagined below them. As we recite the stanza we should visualize ourself transformed into the Ḍākinī Rudrānī (khros.ma) and that our body is transformed into the nectar of Primordial Awareness, a suitable object of offering. As we recite the second stanza we should visualize that by giving away this body cherished by the ego the scared recipients are satisfied. We then think that all our karmic debts have been cleared, that all obstacles of illness and the like have melted away, and that the non-virtuous tendencies and emotional defilements have been purified. By doing so we receive as blessings all the qualities of the objects to whom the offering is made. In conclusion we should remain in a meditative state of non-conceptualization, realizing the object of offering, the offering and offerer to be empty of self-nature.

This Mendicant's practice results in benefits such as the perfection of merit, the overcoming of obstacles to one's life, pacifying of illness and evil spirits and the ability to recognize the Radiant Clarity, or Clear Light, in the intermediary stage between death and the next life.

5. Prostrations

There is no special place assigned to prostrations in this text of the Uncommon Preliminary Practices, but in fact one hundred thousand prostrations are performed as an integral part of it. The actual practice of prostration is found among the seven acts of devotion included in the Unification with the Spiritual Master, the following section and main practice, and it is proper to perform prostrations while reciting the verses of that practice. However these days the full hundred thousand prostrations are done either in combination with the Refuge, Activating the Awakening Mind or the Vajrasattva practice. When making prostrations we should visualize the assembly of the Refuge Objects in the sky above us, and with reverence perform full bodily prostrations while reciting the relevant verses. This should be done with strong devotion and faith towards the objects of prostration, never allowing our mind to wander towards any other object. We can expand the meditation so that we visualize our body being multiplied into as many atoms as there are in the world. We first stand straight and fold our hands together like a lotus blossom. We place them successively at our head, throat and heart, and while thinking that our physical, verbal and mental defilements are purified, we should touch our head, hands and knees to the ground while executing a full bodily prostration. We should rise immediately, and think that our defilements are purified and that we have received the blessings of the Body, Speech, Mind, Qualities and Activity of the Buddhas. We should meditate in this way while performing prostrations with a strong faith and belief.

-3-
The Actual Path

1. Unification with the Spiritual Master (Guru Yoga)

A tantra states, "It is better for a person to remember a Spiritual Master for a moment, than to meditate on one hundred forms of divinities for one hundred thousand aeons." Sarahā, the teacher of Nāgārjuna stated, "The spontaneously arising Primordial Awareness is obviously a product of purification of defilements, accumulation of merit, and of the blessing of realized masters: a spiritual method other than just this should be understood as mistaken."

The practice of Unification with the Spiritual Master is the finest method for realizing the innate wisdom within oneself. It is accomplished through one's own faith and by the grace or blessing of the Spiritual Guide. All Fully Awakened Beings abide inseparably in the expanse of Primordial Awareness, and all are in essence one. The Spiritual Master is the embodiment unifying all wisdom, compassion and power of an Awakened Being. Understanding this with strong devotion and belief will lead to a direct experience of the essence of the path. By these means the emotional defilements are purified and the accumulation of merit and wisdom is perfected. Mixing one's own mind with the mind of the master through the four Tantric Empowerments, and then abiding relaxed in that state, enables the blessings of the Lama to be transferred to one's own mind, and thus one's mind and the mind of the teacher will become inseparable. This is the extraordinary path gaining liberation effortlessly through the realization of the unmodified nature of reality.

The All-knowing Long-chen Rab-jam-pa says in his Gyu-ma Ngal-so (Relaxing in the Illusory Nature), "Merely by practicing devotion to one's teacher one shall easily attain the spiritual stages and paths. If one never departs from the thought of the Spiritual Master, all Fully Awakened Beings will be with you without any separation."

Although this practice is designated as the final part of the Preliminary Practice, it is in fact the most important aspect of all practices.

i. Visualization

To purify all perceptible phenomena into the state of equality and purity is the sublime uniqueness of Tantra. In this case all phenomena are purified into the Pure Land and divinities of Guru Rinpoche, Padmasambhava. One should dissolve the ordinary way of grasping all perceptible phenomena into the expanse of Truth (chos.dbying.; Dharmadhatu), the emptiness of self existent entities, and then imagine them as the Pure Land of the Glorious Copper-colored Mountain, Akaniṣhṭa Tāmtra shri$parvata, which is fully adorned with all symbols and ornamentation. At the center of this palace we should imagine ourself as Vajra Yoginī in appearance and the Ḍākinī Ye-she Tsho-gyäl in nature.

Vajra Yoginī's form may vary according to different traditions. In the text Kun-zang La-ma'i Zhäl-lung, the visualization of Vajra Yoginī is as follows. She is naked, red in color, with flower and bone ornaments. In her right hand she is shaking skull drum (ḍamaru) in the air, signifying awakening from the sleep of ignorance. Her left hand rests on her hip and holds a curved vajra blade, signifying the severing of the three poisons of greed, ignorance and hatred at the root. Her two legs stand in the advancing posture on a lotus and sun seat. Her three eyes look urgently into the heart of Guru Rinpoche. According to the teachings from the great master Jam-yang Khyen-tse'i Wang-po, the variation is that she holds a curved vajra blade in her right hand which signifies cutting off grasping and grasper from the root. Her left hand holds a skull filled with blood, signifying the destruction of the root of birth and death. In the cleft of her left arm she holds a trident of khaṭvaṅga, signifying the inseparability of wisdom and skillful means. She stands on a seat of lotus, sun and corpse in the advancing posture and is adorned with silk and bone ornaments. Her three eyes look into the heart of Guru Rinpoche with devotion.

In visualizing oneself as Vajra Yoginī, the Ḍākinī, there are three purposes: it prepares one as a suitable vessel for receiving Tantric empowerments; it hastens the development of Blissful Emptiness and Wisdom; and it enables one to be accepted as a disciple by Padmasaṃbhava.

While holding the visualization of oneself as Vajra Yoginī according to either of these explanations, or according to specific instructions from one's own teacher, we should visualize, in the sky in front or above one's head, the form of Padmasaṃbhava. He sits in the midst of a large, fully blossomed one hundred thousand-petalled lotus, on a seat of sun and moon, which signify the inseparability of Wisdom and Skillful Means. He is one's principle Lama appearing in the form of Guru Rinpoche or Padmasaṃbhava, with all major and minor marks associated with the perfect form of a Buddha, the embodiment of all the objects of Refuge. He has one face, signifying the realization that all existent things are of "one taste" in the actual state of the Dharma nature. He has two hands, signifying the inseparable relationship between Wisdom and Skillful Means. His complexion is white with a pink hue, signifying the unity of Bliss and Emptiness. He stares with both eyes which signify impartiality in looking upon the world with wisdom and compassion. His youthful appearance signifies freedom from the changes of birth, death and old age. He is wearing a white undergarment (gsang.gos) and a red gown ('dong.ma), signifying the perfection of the Bodhisattva's vehicle. Over these he wears a dark blue tunic (phod.chen) signifying perfection in the practice of Tantra, and over this a red robe (chos.gos) signifying his perfection of the path of the Hināyāna or Shrāvakayāna, and over all these he wears a dark brocade cape, signifying complete accomplishment in all spiritual traditions of Buddhism. He holds in his right hand a five-pronged Vajra scepter at his heart with a threatening mudrā, banishing negative thoughts of a duality between that which is grasped and the grasper. In his left hand he holds a skull, in which is a vessel filled with nectar, signifying the attainment of power over life (tshe. dbang.rig.'dzin). In the cleft of his left arm he holds a trident (khaṭvaṅga), the concealed symbol of his consort, Māndārava, the revealer of Bliss and Emptiness. He wears the hat known as the Lotus Hat signifying that the belongs to the Lotus Family of the Dhyāni Buddha Amitābha. He wears shoes known as Sak-lham, and sits in the playful posture of a king signifying the accomplishment of his own aims and those of others.

Surrounding him in various auras of rainbows, large and small, one should visualize the eight Siddhas of India, the 25 close Tibetan disciples, the Lord of subjects, the three spiritual roots of the Lama, Yidam and Khadro, Dharma Protectors and all objects of Refuge massing like a billowing array of clouds. These divinities should be visualized in a pure land in a state of great luminescence and natural equanimity, appearing, but not having existence in reality. All the forms are clear yet unmixed with the duality of actual existence, like the reflection of the moon in water and a rainbow in the sky.

ii. Invocation and Invitation

This seven line prayer of invocation of the Mind of Guru Rinpoche originated from Guru Rinpoche himself, and was revealed consistently, again and again by earlier and later revealers of the spiritual treasures. If one recites this prayer, Guru Rinpoche himself has promised that he will actually come and instill blessings. There are different meanings of this prayer according to the various levels of capacity of the disciples. On the ordinary level the interpretation is as follows:

> In the northwest country of Uddiyāna
> Is the one born on the pistil of the stem of a lotus
> And endowed with the most marvelous attainments,
> Renowned as the Lotus-Born One, Padmasaṃbhava,
> And surrounded by a retinue of many Ḍākinīs:
> I will practice by following you;
> Please come forth to grace me with your inspiration.
> GURU PADMA SIDDHI HŪṂ;

This is a direct expression of the method for practicing the prayer in relation to Guru Rinpoche's appearance in this world as a perfect body of Emanation or Nirmāṇakāya. In actuality he is not separable from the Primordial Buddha, Samantabhadra, who is, from the very beginning, fully liberated in the state of the self-originated Dharmakāya. Without moving from the expanse of the Dharmakāya, he is spontaneously accomplished in the state of the Saṃbhogakāya which is endowed with five certain qualities. He is the spontaneous arising of unimaginably various miraculous manifestations, all of which are their own reflection of his compassion. This is the actual way in which Guru Rinpoche abides and appears, and is the display which is exclusively perceived by a fully awakened being.

For the ordinary disciples who have good fortune, he took birth as the Lotus Born One in the form of Padmasaṃbhava, Guru Rinpoche. During his life he manifested himself to his disciples in forms appropriate to the occasion such as one of the eight emanations of the guru (gu.ru.mtshan.brgyad). It was in one of these forms that he performed innumerable miracles with his psychic powers and tantric attainments (dngos.grub; siddhi) and displayed various acts of learning, teaching and debate to his disciples—men and women, ordinary and highly realized beings, non-humans as well as spirits—in his own country of Uddiyāna (N. W. Pakistan), in

India and in Tibet. This level of interpretation is the general way of understanding the implication of these seven lines when praying to this extraordinary object of devotion.

That interpretation of these lines is as follows:

The prayer begins with the seed syllable HŪṂ—the invocation of the mind of Guru Rinpoche, the mind of all the Buddhas, the indicator of the self-arisen primordial wisdom. The first line speaks of his origin in the land North west of India, the country of Uddiyāna, the land of Ḍākinis and the Dhamakoṣha Lake. The second refers to his miraculous birth on the pistil of the stem of a lotus. At that time all the qualities and blessings of the three mystic aspects of a Buddha's body, speech and mind came together in the form of the seed syllable HRĪ and dissolved into the heart of Amitabha Buddha. From his heart they emanated as five colored rays of light and lit upon the pistil of the lotus. There they transformed into Guru Rinpoche and he thus took birth. The third line shows that he spontaneously accomplished the two-fold benefit for himself and others and exhibited a marvelous life by such means as his eight emanations. He achieved the supreme attainment, the unification with Dorje-chang (Vajradhara). His name, in the fourth line, is renowned as the Lotus-born, Padmasaṃbhava. And in the fifth line, he is surrounded by retinues of many Ḍākās (mkha'. 'gro) and Ḍākinīs (mkha'. 'gro.ma), the inspirational emanations of tantric energy and wisdom.

At the conclusion in the sixth and seventh lines one should pray with the three kinds of faith—faith which is pure and cleanses the mind (dang.ba'i.dad.pa), faith which is inspirational and desirous of accomplishing the same attainment as the object of such devotion ('dod.pa'i.dad.pa) and faith which is grounded in full confidence in the unequalled qualities of the object of faith (yid.ches.kyi.dad.pa). Here we pray "O protector, in following you I will practice" with the intention of emulating Guru Rinpoche and achieving inseparability with him, or simply to develop confidence and conviction in the path. In the last line, keeping in mind that we and all sentient beings are sunk in the ocean of the three sufferings of birth, ageing and death, we request Guru Rinpoche, who is wise, compassionate and powerful, to "please come forth to grace me with your inspirational blessings of your body, speech and mind," transforming ours just as iron is transmuted into gold.

The concluding mantra of Padmasambhava for invoking his

blessings has the following meaning: Guru, or Lama in Tibetan, the Spiritual Master, means one who is "weighty" or "heavy" with excellent qualities, and also means one to whom no one is superior—one who is peerless; Padma is the first name of Guru Rinpoche; siddhi are the common and uncommon spiritual attainments we wish to obtain; and HŪṂ means the supplication to bestow these attainments. Thus the whole mantra means "O Guru, bestow the spiritual attainments."

Although this is the general interpretation of these seven lines and mantra, there are deeper meanings according to the level of one's intelligence and attainment. There is the hidden meaning: first according to the Way of Liberation (grol.lam) which reflects the tantric understanding of emptiness; second according to the Way of Skillful Means (thabs. lam) which reflects the tantric methods of practice such as the meaning according to the general process of the Completing Stage (rdzogs.rim) using the inner psychic system; and third is the meaning according to the specific teaching of the Innermost Essence, the practice of Instantaneous Presence (thod.rgal) in the State. Beyond this these seven lines can be interpreted according to the realization of the actual accomplishment of the practice. These levels are disclosed by one's Spiritual Master and accommodate the various natures, intellects and capacities of the disciples. It is appropriate to recite it according to one's level of realization.

One should recite it with a sweet devotional melody, imagining that the actual divinities came from the Pure Land of the Copper-colored Mountain like snowflakes falling from the sky and merge with their visualized counterparts like the snowflakes falling upon water. The visualization becomes very bright, emitting rays of light with tremendous intensity. Thereupon one should develop deep faith that they are in fact the embodiment of all the wisdom, compassion and power of the Fully Awakened Beings.

iii. The Seven Aspects of Devotion for the Accumulation of Merit

In order to develop within oneself the extraordinary realizations of the spiritual stages and paths, it is necessary to dispel unfavorable conditions and to activate those which are favorable. This leads to the attainment of the common and uncommon extraordinary powers. With this aim in view, one should purify mental defilements within the context of aid from the assembly of Refuge objects of the most excellent path of Tantra. Imagining the assembly in one's mind's eye, one should engage in methods for purification and accumulation by the seven aspects of devotional practice.

With prostration, visualize one's own body multiplied to the number of atoms in the world together with all sentient beings, and without any pride one should perform full prostrations devoting body, speech and mind to the objects of Refuge.

The practice of offering involves actual offerings of those which are pleasingly and cleanly arranged, and visualized offering, which are all the wealth of the gods and materials which are pleasing to the senses throughout the world, filling the sky, together with numerous offering goddesses who hold aloft exquisite arrays of offerings. These should then be visualized as being offered to the assembly without any trace of attachment and avarice or hypocrisy. One should consider that the recipients are pleased with the quality of this offering.

With confession, we should lay bare all wrongdoings that we and all other beings have accumulated throughout the three times in actions of our body, speech and mind. This should be done with a strong feeling of repentance and remorse, and an intention to turn away from committing such actions again. We should visualize that by confessing, rays of light shine forth from the objects of Refuge, touch the bodies of all sentient beings, and purify us from all defilements as if washed away by water. In accordance with a special form of confession, all defilements are purified by relaxing in the state of realization of luminescence or radiant clarity, free from conceptualization.

When we rejoice, we should rejoice in the accumulation of virtues on both the relative and ultimate level of oneself and others, without any trace of jealousy.

To all the Buddhas, Bodhisattvas and spiritual teachers dwelling in the ten directions, one should request that they set in motion the wheel of Dharma of the great, medium and lower vehicles, in accordance with the varying capacities and intellects of the disciples. We should wish that these teachings are given ceaselessly, without any interruption.

We should request that the Fully Awakened Beings, their spiritual sons and all realized teachers do not leave this world for the state of Nirvāṇa, and that they remain within the world for the sake of beings until all sentient beings have attained Buddhahood and cyclic existence has been emptied.

In the last of these seven practices, we should dedicate the merit of ourselves and others which has been accumulated throughout time, in order that all sentient beings may enjoy happiness and virtue, finally attaining the state of the All-knowing Primordial Protector. This we should do without hoping for recompense or personal gain from such action, in accordance with the way in which Mañjushri and other Bodhisattvas distribute their merit.

After all defilements and unfavorable conditions have been purified, and spiritual merit and favorable conditions for achieving Liberation have been accumulated, the rain of blessings of the Refuge Lama is required so that the corps of the achievement of Liberation and the state of Omniscience may grow. To attract the rainfilled cloud of bliss it is necessary to practice invocation with a strong faith through the "wind of prayer".

iv. Invocation

With the mind focused single-pointedly in prayer, one should pray to Guru Rinpoche, who is seen as inseparable from one's own Root Lama—the united body of Wisdom, Compassion and Power of all Buddhas—thinking: "I and others who are sunk deep in the ocean of cyclic existence have no guide except you; we depend upon you in this life and the next. Please always watch over us with your kindness." This prayer should be performed with full and deep consideration of its meaning, so that tears come to our eyes and the hairs stand up on our body.

v. The Mantra Recitation

At the end of this prayer one should repeat the essence of the heart of the prayer known as "Siddhi". All the outer manifestations of saṃsara should be recognized as the emanation of the pure realm of Guru Rinpoche, the Glorious Copper-colored Mountain; all beings should be seen as Ḍākās and Ḍākinīs; all sounds should be heard as the Siddhi mantra; and all reflections of mind should be recognized as being self-liberated from the very beginning. The significance of the mantra is as follows:

OṂ ĀH HŪṂ: These are the seeds of the vajra body, speech and mind of all the Buddhas.

VAJRA: The body of Truth, the Dharmakāya, which in its adamantine nature is not able to be affected by the conceptualizing of characteristic thoughts.

GURU: The perfect body of Complete Enjoyment, the Saṃbhogakāya, signifies that this visionary state is weighty with the heavy abundance of enlightened qualities.

PADMA: The perfect body of Emanation, the Nirmāṇakāya, is in the nature of discriminating awareness arising in the Speech—Padma family.

By praying to Guru Rinpoche, who is the embodiment of these three perfect bodies, then,

SIDDHI: All the common and uncommon attainments,

HŪṂ: May be bestowed in my mind immediately.

2. Prayers to the Lamas of the Lineage

This prayer is a condensation of a prayer to all the Lamas of the lineage beginning with Kuntu Zangpo, passing through Vajrasattva, Garab Dorje, Srīsiṅha and so forth to Guru Rinpoche and his disciples, and from them through Long-Chen Rab-jam-pa, Jig-me Lingpa, Do-drup Chen, Gyal-wa'i Nyu-gu and so forth, all the way down to one's own Root Lama. More lengthy prayers to the lineage can be added depending on instructions given by one's own teacher.

Aspirational Prayers

With these aspirations we direct our mind towards the attainment of the spiritual stages, paths and results of the Dzog-chen practice. For those relating to this life, we should think, "May I develop renunciation, the wish to gain liberation from cyclic existence; may I be suitably connected with a Tantric Master; may his realization be transferred to my mind; may everything be perceived as arising as the three Vajras—namely the appearances as divine, sounds as mantra and the mind as Dharmakāya; and may I perfect the four mystical visions."

Following this is a prayer which relates to the passage between death and the next life. Here we express the aspiration that if we do not achieve liberation in this life, "may the death-trance arise as Primordial Wisdom, and the vision of the Intermediate State be liberated as the Saṃbhogakaya; may I perfect the experiences of the Essence (ngo.bo) and its manifestation (rang.bzhin) by the path of Treg-cho (khregs.chod) and Tho-gal (thod.rgal), and thus in the Intermediate State attain liberation like a child climbing into his mother's lap."

If we do not achieve liberation then, with the support of the five practices for attaining Buddhahood without meditation (namely the practice of Chakras or diagrams, which leads to liberation through seeing; that of Nectar, which gives liberation through hearing; that of Mantra, which gives liberation through tasting; and that of Mudrā, which gives liberation through touching and that of Transference of consciousness, which leads to liberation through recollecting) we should wish, "May I then gain rebirth as a Nirmāṇakāya in a Pure realm and attain liberation thereby receiving Mahāyāna teachings. Thus may I perform service for others without any effort." We should pray to achieve all the above aspirations by the power of the Ultimate Truth.

3. Receiving the Four Empowerments

Through praying in such a way the minds of the Refuge Objects have been invoked, and we should visualize that all the surrounding retinue dissolve into Guru Rinpoche, and that his glory of Wisdom and Power increases tremendously. Rays of light are then emitted from his three sacred places, and they enter oneself at the same three points so that the Four Tantric Empowerments are obtained, the four defilements are purified and the state of the four Perfect Bodies is actualized. At the end we should mix our own mind with the mind of Guru Rinpoche and relax in that state.

In conclusion, we should dissolve the visualization with a feeling of strong devotion, and from this dissolution comes a warm red ray of light from Guru Rinpoche's heart. It dissolves into our own heart and we become a red body of light which then dissolves into Guru Rinpoche's heart. We should be at ease in that state without reflection or conceptualization for as long as possible.

4. Dedication

Distribution of merit for the benefit of others should be done with kindness, compassion and the altruistic attitude of Awakening Mind, so that we wish all sentient beings may, by these good actions, gain happiness and the ultimate attainment of Enlightenment. If one dedicates merit for the ultimate benefit of others the virtues will never decrease, they will only increase. It is an immensely powerful, skillful means for perfecting one's own accumulation of goodness. The exceptional means of dedicating merit is to do so in conjunction with the realization of their non-reality—

without the practice being defiled by attachment to any reality in the merit to be dedicated, in the objects to whom it is being dedicated and in the purpose for which it is dedicated. If one aspires to achieve such a purpose supported by any sacred object and the cause of merit—good actions—they will fulfill one's wishes. Therefore, from the depths of one's heart, one should make vast aspirations for the achievement of happiness, good fortune and birth in higher realms of existence, and finally for the attainment of the Fully Awakened state both by oneself and others.

Part - III

The Nine Yanas[28]

A Guide to the Approaches to Enlightenment

Generally the wide variety of traditions and paths in Buddhism reflects the numerous dispositions and capacities of its followers. Within the Nyingma tradition they are all synthesized into nine, of which the Dzog-chen of Atiyoga is the supreme, the others being considered as the tools or adjuncts to this. Just as there are disciples at varying stages of spiritual development, there are also varying levels of spiritual paths, and these paths reflect the type of practice which is emphasized at such levels.

Out of the nine vehicles, or Yānas, the first and the second, that of the Hearers, Shrāvakas, and that of the solitary Realizers, the Pratyekabuddhas, both belong to the Lesser Vehicle or Hināyāna. Their training consists mainly of cultivating pure moral discipline. The third is the vehicle of the Bodhisattva, the Awakening Warrior. Here the practitioner mainly cultivates the Awakening Mind, the altruistic thought to bring ultimate benefit to others. This way and the successive vehicles belong to the Greater Vehicle or Mahāyāna. These first three Yānas are known as Causal Vehicles, because the practice is directed towards those activities which act as a cause for the attainment of Enlightenment. They are also known respectively as the lower, middle and higher spiritual paths of beings on the ordinary level of capability. The last six vehicles, which include the Action or Kriyā, Performance or Caryā and the yoga Tantras, and the Mahā, Anu and Ati Yogas, are all part of the Tantric Path. They mainly involve training in the purification of the appearances of existence (snang.srid). The first three are known as the external tantras, the last three as the internal ones. These are also known as the Resultant Vehicles because the practice primarily centers on the result of the path itself being taken as the practice. This is the path for those of exceptional ability, who are endowed with excellent or superlative capacity.

In the Tantra known as Heruka Kalpo it states:

"By the Causal Vehicle it can be understood
That the mind is the cause of Buddhahood.

By the Resultant Vehicle meditate
That the mind itself (sems.nyid) is Buddhahood."

In the Causal vehicles the mind will accumulate the mental and physical merit, and by practicing the path of the Bodhisattva's conduct the result will be obtained. Thus it is considered that the mind is just the cause of the result and that the cause and result precede and follow one another. Thus they are known as the Causal Vehicles.

The six vehicles of the Tantras are viewed in such a way that the essence of the mind is the final attainment or the result, and that this has been within oneself from the very beginning, yet is covered by fleeting defilements and negativities. If these are uncovered and the recognition of one's own self-nature arises, that is the attainment of the ultimate result. So in this case there is no discrimination of "preceding and following" in the idea normally associated with cause and result. Therefore it is called the Resultant Vehicle. These six higher vehicles are more extraordinary than the lower ones by virtue of the wide variety of profound and rapid skillful means associated with their practice.

1. The Three Causal Vehicles

i. Shrāvakayāna or The Way of the Hearers

View: With regard to the two kinds of lack of self-identity or selflessness they understand the lack of self-identity in personalities (gang.zag.gi.bdag.med; pudgalanairātma), yet they uphold the ultimate reality of dimensionless atoms and the shortest, indivisible moments of consciousness as an example of the self-identity of phenomena (chos.kyi.bdag; dharmātma).

Aim: The wish to attain peace and happiness for oneself.

Practice: The observance of any one of the eight (or seven) vows of individual liberation (so.sor.thar.pa; pratimokṣha). These are: i) Upavāsatha-shīla, the precepts kept on lunar observance days; ii) Upāsakā-shīla, male devotees' precepts; iii) Upāsikā-shīla, female devotees' precepts; iv) Shramaṇera-shīla, male novices' precepts; v) Shramaṇerikā-shīla, female novices' precepts; vi) Shīkshāmaṇa-shīla, training precepts for female probationers; vii) Bhikṣhu-shīla, fully ordained monks' precepts; viii) Bhikṣhu-ṇī-shīla, fully ordained nuns' precepts.

Meditation: Making the mind and body fit for practice by the meditation of tranquillity or calm abiding (zhi.gnas; shamatha), such as meditation on repulsiveness as an antidote to desire, concentrating on the exhalation and inhalation of breath to subdue discursive thoughts and the four close contemplations on form, feeling, consciousness and phenomena and so forth. They follow this with vivid insight meditation (lhag.mthong; vipashyanā) on the Four Noble Truths with their 16 aspects such as impermanence and so forth. Wisdom is attained by meditating on the understanding of suffering as an illness, rejecting the cause of suffering as the cause of an illness, attaining the cessation of suffering like the cure of an illness, and depending on the spiritual path as one depends on medicine which is the antidote to an illness.

Result: There are four stages of the result: that of a stream-enterer, a once-returner, a never-returner and an Arhat (lit.: One who has "subdued the enemy" of conflicting emotions). Each of these stages has two phases, namely the initial or entrance stage, and the result. Thus there are eight stages of result in all.

ii. Pratyekabuddhayāna or the Way of the Solitary Realizers, the Self-Enlightened or Silent Buddhas.

View: The Pratyekabuddha understands the absence of a self in personalities as well as that related to mental events. They understand the lack of self-identity in phenomenal objects but hold the view that the smallest moment of consciousness is ultimately real.

Aim: To achieve one's own enlightenment by one's own efforts.

Practice: To observe any one of the vows of individual liberation.

Meditation: To meditate on tranquil abiding or shamatha, and upon the Four Noble Truths with their 16 aspects as followed in the Shrāvaka-yāna. In addition they meditate on the 12 links in the chain of interdependent origination (rten.'byung; pratītyasamutpāda) in successive and reverse orders.

Result: After accumulating virtue for one hundred aeons, the rhinoceros-like Pratyekabuddha will complete "on one seat" the attainments from the "heat" stage of the Path of Endeavor (sbyor.lam; prayogamārga) until Arhathood, on the stage of no more learning (mi.slob.lam; ashaikṣhamārga).

iii. Bodhisattvayāna

View: The Bodhisattva reaches the conclusion that all phenomena are without any self identity.

Aim: The urge to attain the fully awakened state of being for the benefit of others.

Practice: They practice the six transcending perfections of giving, ethical discipline, patience, diligence, meditative stability, and discriminating intelligence or wisdom, as well as developing the four qualities for attracting disciples (bsdu.dngos. bzhi); giving (byin.pa), gentle speech (snyan.smra), practice according to the meaning of the Dharma (don.mthun) and encouraging others to act according to the meaning (don.spyod)

Meditation: In the four paths of training, meditation on the meaning of the dual lack of self-identity and the 37 wings of enlightenment. These 37 aspects of the path are as follows: the four foundations of mindfulness (dran.pa. nye.bar.bzhag.pa.bzhi), the four perfect abandonments (yang.dag.spang.ba.bzhi), the four miraculous powers (rdzu.'phrul.gyi.rkang.pa.bzhi), the five faculties (dbang.po.lnga), the five forces (stobs.lnga), the seven branches of enlightenment (byang.chub.kyi.yan. lag.bdun) and the eight-fold Noble Path ('phags.lam. yan.lag.brgyad).

Result: After three measureless aeons the Bodhisattva will attain for the sake of himself the fully awakened state, the Dharmakāya, and for the benefit of others until cyclic existence is ended, he shall appear and act for the sake of sentient beings by means of the two perfect bodies of form, that of the Saṃbhogakāya and the Nirmāṇkāya.

2. The Six Resultant Vehicles

The practice of the Tantric path is extraordinary in comparison to the general approach of the Sūtra by virtue of a number of distinguishing features. The text known as the Lamp of the Three Techniques (tshul.gsum.gron.me) states:

> The aim is the same but there is no delusion;
> There are many skillful means and no difficulties;
> It is for people of sharp intellect;
> Hence the Tantrayāna is especially noble.

The goal is the same as the general practice of sūtra, being only the attainment of a fully awakened state of being, yet in the way of attainment, according to tantra, all appearances of cyclic existence are perceived as naturally pure and are to be used as means of supporting the practitioner on the path. Thus, since all phenomena are perceived as primordially pure because the result of the path is taken as the practice, there are no dualistic defilements as there are in the ordinary causal vehicles, in which the acceptance of certain practices and the avoidance of others is a fundamental part of the path. Tantra utilizes many skillful means which are employed in accordance with the specific psychological capacity of the practitioner, and so it avoids the difficulties associated with the sūtra practices such as giving one's body to others. The tantric path is for people of sharp intelligence and a predisposition towards its practice.

In order to engage in Vajrayāna it is essential to have direct contact with a Tantric Master, and to recognize him as the complete master (khyab.bdag) of all spheres of tantric practice. By receiving the full empowerment, initiation and teachings from him, it becomes possible for the mind to be liberated within this lifetime. The entrance to Tantric practice is the empowerment (dbang.; abhiṣhekha) which involves, according to the specific level of the tantric practice, various rituals and visualizations. It is inappropriate to attempt the practice of Tantra without receiving such initiation. This carries with it a number of commitments, the first being that one must observe the precepts associated with the practice (dam. tshig; samāya) without transgressing them. One must also engage in the actual practice of the tantric maṇḍala, which involves two stages, the visualization process (bskyed.rim; utpattikrama) and the process of completion (rdzogs.rim; sampannakrama), involving the recitation of mystical formulae, the practice of a specific method for accomplishment (sgrub. thabs; sādhana) and the complete familiarization with this in meditation. In this way one should complete the various stages and the spiritual paths, thereby attaining the ultimate result. This is the general way of practicing Tantra.

i. The Three External Tantras

A Nyingma text known as the Self-arising Tantra (rang.shar) states: "There are three external tantras: Kriyā, Caryā and Yoga."

(a) Kriyā or Action Tantra (bya.rgyud)

View: In reality all things are perceived as the same, in that appearance and emptiness are an inseparable truth (snang.stong.bden.pa.dbyer.med). However, on the relative level of practice, the divinity or meditational deity is related to in the same way by the practitioner as a servant relates to his master or lord.

Practice: Mainly involves the performance of ritual actions of the body and speech such as washing and cleaning oneself and one's abode. It also involves a lot of details concerning proper and improper foods.

Meditation: In the ordinary practice of Kriyā Tantra one does not visualize oneself as divine or as the divinity, but in a special form of the practice the devotee imagines himself as a divinity by way of the six "divinities", which include meditation on the divine state of thusness or emptiness (de.nyid.stong.pa'i.lha). Generally the practitioner visualizes before himself the deity, and invites it to be present as a servant would a lord by making offerings and singing praises. He or she then concentrates on visualizing the deity's body, speech and mind, the celestial palaces, the spreading and contracting of rays of light from the deity and thereby receives the blessings of the deity through supplication, recitation and meditative stability.

Result: The final result after seven or 16 lives is the attainment of the "Vajra-Holder of the Three Knowledges" (rigs.gsum.rdo.rje.'dzin.pa).

(b) Caryā Tantra or Upa Yoga Tantra (spyod.rgyud)

The view in this case is the same as in the following tantra, the Yoga Tantra, whereas the practice is very similar to that of the Kriyā Tantra.

Meditation: The deity is visualized in front of oneself, and the practitioner also visualizes himself or herself as divine, so that the relationship is similar to that of a brother, sister or a friend. The method of practice then involves recitation of mantra and the stabilization of one's concentration. In this case there are two kinds of meditation, the yoga with signs and the yoga without. That with signs involves the stabilization of mind by concentrating one-pointedly on the deity, the letters of the mantra (in the heart), the gestures or mudrās and the form perceived in visualization. The signless yoga avoids the concentration on such characteristics and involves leaving the mind to remain in the state of ultimate truth.

Result: The attainment of the state of Vajradhara (rdo.rje. 'dzin.pa) within seven lives.

(c) Yoga Tantra (rnal.'byor.rgyud)

View: In ultimate reality all things are naturally free from the signs of mental projections (spros.mtshan. dang.bral.ba), thereby being radiant clarity and emptiness (od.gsal.stong.pa.nyid). On the relative level all appearances are regarded as maṇḍalas of the divinities and the inspirational blessing of truth itself (chos.nyid.kyi.byin.rlabs)

Practice: The practitioner looks upon external activities such as cleaning and eating specific foods as merely the support for the practice and mainly concentrates on practicing for the benefit of others by dwelling in the yoga of the divinity (lha'i.rnal.'byor).

Meditation: Again there are two aspects, the yoga with and without signs. The yoga with signs consists of visualizing oneself in the form of the deity by means of the five perfect qualities of enlightenment (mngon.byang). These are as follows: the perfection of the lunar seat represents the pure realm; the perfection of the seed syllables represents the speech of the deity; the perfection of the symbolic instruments held by the deities represents the mind of the deity; the perfection of complete form of the deity represents the maṇḍala of the deity and the perfection of wisdom—deity or jñanasattva, being visualized within the heart of the deity, represents the essence or wisdom of the deity. The practice also involves the four miraculous manifestations. These are known as follows: i) the miracle of the meditative concentration which is the display about the deity's retinue; ii) the miracle of initiation which is the initiation itself; iii) the miracle of the blessing is the sealing of the practice by means of a mudrā; and iv) the miracle of offering is the practice involving offering, praising, and reciting mantras. One then summons the deity and absorbs him or her into oneself, binding the deity by means of the four mudrās, and after performing the offering, praises, and mantra recitations in the actual practice, the deity is released and one bids the deity farewell while requesting him or her to dwell in the enlightened state. The yoga without signs involves meditating directly on the state of just that itself or tathatā (de.kho.na.nyid), the non-dual nature of the ultimate truth; the blessing of which, here, is that non-duality is inseparable from the appearance of the divinities which are in themselves manifestations of supreme wisdom.

Result: Within three lifetimes one shall attain Buddhahood in the realm of the Beautiful Array (stug.po.bkod.pa).

ii. The three Internal Tantras

In the Self-arising Tantra it is stated, "Three are considered inner tantras: Mahā, Anu and Ati." In brief, the qualities that make the inner tantras more extraordinary than the outer ones are as follows:

First of all, in the initiation the external tantras are mainly centered on the initiation of the Vase (bum.dbang) whereas the inner tantras have in addition three other initiations, the Secret (gsang.dbang), the Wisdom (shes.rab.ye.shes.kyi.dbang) and the Verbal initiations (tshig.dbang). As regards the view, the outer tantras maintain the distinction between the two truths, whereas the inner ones uphold their inseparable identity. With meditation, in the inner tantras the view is upheld that all things are equal in purity, thus avoiding any duality of rejection or acceptance. Without renouncing any of the three poisons of desire, aggression and ignorance, they make use of them as the path so that desire is taken as the union of bliss and emptiness, hatred as the union of clarity and emptiness, and ignorance as the union of awareness and emptiness. They practice the meditation of the two stages of tantra without any partiality towards one over the other. The visualization in the inner tantras involves oneself as the deity in union with the consort (yab.yum) which indicates the complete union of skillful means and wisdom. The external tantras cannot be practiced in such a way.

Furthermore, in the practice of the inner tantras the five meats of cow, dog, elephant, horse and man, together with the five nectars of excrement, brains, semen, blood and urine are used without any duality such as their acceptance or rejection. Such object involved in the practice cannot be found in the practice of the outer tantras. It is by practicing the inner tantras that the resultant state of enlightenment can be achieved in this very life.

(a) Mahā Yoga

These are also known as the Father Tantras (pha.rgyud) and center primarily on elaborate visualizations and various other activities of somewhat secondary importance. Emphasis in meditation is placed on realizing the illusory body (rgyu.lus; māyādeha) as being the ultimate wisdom in terms of the skillful means of appearance, the completion process of the inner energy (rlung.gi.rdzogs.rim) and the action of extraordinary behavior (mngon.spyod.kyi.las) for subduing enemies of the Dharma. This practice is primarily for an individual who has a greater predominance of anger or aggression and discriminating thoughts.

View: The view of the ultimate truth is that all things are the essence of mind and that appearance and emptiness are inseparable in the realm of the Dharmakāya. The relative truth is the power of this to manifest itself so that all thoughts, speech and action are the self-appearance of the maṇḍala of the Vajra Body, Speech and Mind.

Practice: The practice of the Father Tantras involves utilizing by skillful means, and without attachment to anything, the objects throughout cyclic existence, enjoying them and utilizing them in the practice without rejecting or accepting anything, including such objects as the five meats and nectars.

Meditation: Meditation is focused on the non-dualistic supreme wisdom of bliss, clarity and non-conceptuality by purifying all appearances as divinities and their environments and to visualize the psycho-physical constituents (phung.po.lnga; skandhas), the sensory spheres (khams; dhātu) and the sensory entrances (skye.mched; ayatana) as divine.

Result: The achievement of the fully Awakened state of being in this very lifetime.

(b) Anu Yoga Tantra

The Anu Yoga Tantra is also known as the Mother Tantra (ma.rgyud) and in tantras of this classification, rather than the emphasis being placed on the skillful means involved in the development process, the practitioner meditates primarily on the completion process (rdzogs.rim). The practice thus emphasizes the cultivation of the discriminating wisdom which cognizes emptiness. This is done by means of the yoga of radiant clarity, and the method of integrating skillful means is to utilize the bliss attained through sexual practice. From the four actions which may be undertaken in tantric practice, namely that of pacification, expansion, power and wrathfulness, here the emphasis is mainly on that of power. This tantra is directed more to an individual who has a predominance of desire and who likes the mind to be stabilized (sems.gnas.pa.la.dga'.ba) and who also has the ability to engage in the physical practices.

View: The practitioner perceives everything arising as the three maṇḍalas. The maṇḍala of the nature of everything is spontaneously manifest and is seen as Samantabhadra, the masculine counterpart in the practice. That this is empty of attachment to extreme views is perceived as the primordial maṇḍala which has existed from the very beginning and is manifest as Samantabhadrī, the female counterpart of the practice. That both of them in nature abide in the essence of union without separation or joining is perceived as the maṇḍala of Bodhicitta. The outcome of this total integration is great bliss, and is conceived as the son of the mystical union.

Practice: The practice mainly centers on understanding the essence of oneness, or a holistic view.

Meditation: In meditation one cultivates the awareness that the world and all beings have been enlightened in the maṇḍalas of deities from the very beginning. There is less emphasis on visualization and more on the perfection of bliss, clarity and non-conceptuality by means of the yogas of the psychic veins, semen and psychic energy (rtsa.thig.rlung.gi.rnal.'byor).

There are two main aspects to meditation in Anu Yoga, the paths of liberation and skillful means. In the path of liberation one meditates on the ultimate significance of reality by cultivating the primordial awareness which is not disturbed by conceptualizing thoughts (rnam.par.mi.rtog.pa'i.ye.shes). In accordance with the "letter" one meditates by reciting the mantras for visualization and visualizing the world and the beings as maṇḍalas of divinities, arising within one's field of perception spontaneously like fish leaping out of the river. In the path of skillful means the meditation involves developing the co-emergent primordial awareness (lhan.skyes.kyi.ye.shes) by means of either using the four or six psychic centers (`khor.lo; cakras) of the "upper doors" of the head, throat, heart, navel, stomach and sexual psychic centers, which is a gradual way, or by using the union of the "lower doors" which is the instantaneous way.

Result: The attainment of complete enlightenment within the space of one lifetime.

Ati Yoga

This is also known as the Great Completion (rdzogs.pa.chen.po; Mahāsandhi) and is specially characterized by being known as the great primordial wisdom of the equality of purity, the naturally arisen primordial wisdom free from assumptions and projections, the final nature of all things and the summit of all spiritual vehicles. This is considered the most fitting practice to discipline people of a greater predominance of ignorance and active mind.

View: The practitioner concludes that everything within the realm of both cyclic existence and the state beyond sorrow, saṃsāra and nirvāṇa, is in the nature of the great primordial wisdom of the spontaneously arising Dharmakāya or perfect body of truth. All things are only appearances in the mind. Their existence is false because in reality their apparent nature is nonexistent. All things within the world are of the same nature without any discrimination. They have been this way from the beginning of time and are in the nature of the three perfect bodies (sku.gsum; trikāya). The empty essence of the mind itself is the Dharmakāya, the radiant, clear nature of the mind is the Saṃbhogakāya and the unimpeded universal compassion of the mind is the Nirmāṇakāya (ngo.bo.stong.pa.chos.sku; rang.bzhin.gsal.ba.longs.sku; thugs.rje.'gags.med. sprul.sku)

Practice: The Dzog-chen practice encompasses the experience of everything without acceptance or rejection, by perceiving all that appears as activities of truth itself or the Dharma essence (chos.nyid;dharmatā).

Meditation: Dzog-chen is practiced according to three categories of teachings in the tantras: i) the Mind Category (sems.sde) mainly involves revealing, by means of analysis, the essential nature of the self-awareness of the Dharmakāya, ii) the Expansive Category (klong.sde) centers on showing the meditation of abiding effortlessly in the state of reality itself or the Dharma essence, iii) the Concealed Instruction Category (man.ngag.sde) concentrates on analyzing the primordial awareness of the self-existent luminescence, or radiant clarity, while remaining in the state of reality itself, a state of detachment from acceptance or rejection which is free from the very beginning of time.

Long-chen Rab-jam-pa, in his Treasury of Tenets, divides the three categories of the Dzog-chen tantras in the following way:

> In Sem-de all the various appearances are the play of the mind, just as in the single face of a

> mirror various colors can appear. In Long-de the self-arising primordial awareness and all the various phenomena which arise from its manifestative power are liberated and pure from the beginning. Thus even the mind and the play of appearances of the mind do not exist in truth. In Man-ngag-de one is not to remain in mental analysis but is to make the nature spontaneously clear or self-evident, and to pierce to the point (to get to the very heart of the essential understanding) like the fire-probe treatment.

Accordingly one should first make the mind receptive by following the preliminary practices. Then one should obtain the "introduction to intrinsic awareness" by means of the initiation of awareness (rig.pa'i.tsal.dbang). Following this one should practice the actual path which in Dzog-chen means first remaining without moving from the state of the actual unmodified meaning of the originally pure "cutting to the essence" (khregs.chod). Secondly one follows the method of "instantaneous arrival" or Thögäl (thod.rgal), which involves six points of spontaneous accomplishment. These relate to the i) body, ii) speech, iii) mind, iv) the "rising door" or eyes, v) the "rising ground" or object, and vi) the "breathing awareness". In this practice the delusions are purified into the original ground and the four visions are perfected. These are: i) the direct perception of truth itself, ii) the development of experiences and sensations, iii) arriving at an understanding of the measure of intrinsic awareness or Rig-pa, and iv) dissolving everything into reality itself or Dharmatā. One first perceives the meaning of the bare perception of pure awareness (rig.pa.mngon.sum), then enhances it, which will lead to the arrival at an understanding of the true state of being, until finally all delusory appearances of everything are exhausted or purified into the vast expanse of reality itself. Upon reaching this stage one will attain the four confidences, namely confidence of no fear of hell, no expectation of results,

	no expectation of attainment and purifying happiness and enjoyment in the essential sameness.
Result:	From this point onwards all will be perfected and one will dwell in the state of spontaneous perfection (lhun.rdzogs), the state of the primordial Buddha Samantabhadra, and one will be liberated in the state of primordial purity.

Notes

1. dkon.mchog.gsum; tri-ratna.
2. bDe.bar.gshegs.pa; Sugata.
3. rtsa.ba.gsum.
4. Physical channels (rsta; nāḍī); energy winds (rlung; vāyu); seminal essence (thig.le; bindu).
5. Essence (ngo.bo;svabhāva); nature (rang.bzhin; prakṛiti); compassion (thugs.rje; karuṇā).
6. Byang.chub.snying.po; Bodhimaṇḍa.
7. Ngal.gso. The anxiety-free state of Buddhahood.
8. Rang.rig.'od.gsal.
9. Tshad.med.bzhi.
10. Long.spyod.rdzogs.pa'i.sku; Saṃbhogakāya.
11. Khams.gsum; triloka or tridhātu. They are (1) the desire realm ('dod.khams; kāmadhātu), (2) the form realm (gzugs.khams; rūpadhātu), and (3) the formless realm (gzugs.med.khams; arūpadhātu).
12. Khros.ma.
13. The body, speech and mind—in other words, the three media of actions.
14. All appearances are perfected as deities, all sounds are purified as mantras and all thoughts are ripened into the Dharmakāya, the perfect body of truth.
15. Rig.pa'i.gdangs.
16. Chos.nyid; dharmatā.
17. mngon.sum.
18. rig.stsal.
19. khregs.chod.
20. thod.rgal.
21. The five practices are those granting liberation through just seeing the cakras, by hearing the mantra, by tasting the nectar, by touching the mudrā, or by recollecting the po-wa transference of consciousness.
22. The five pure realms are the Vajra Realm in the east, the Padma in the west, the Ratna in the south, the Karma in the north and the Buddha in the center of the maṇḍala.
23. The abode of Guru Rinpoche, the Glorious Copper-colored Mountain.

24. rDzogs.smin.sbyang.gsum.
25. The practice of the "Chaṅḍali" inner heat, the "tu-mo".
26. The ālaya (kun.gzhi) is the storehouse or the basis of the traces and causation of virtuous and unvirtuous deeds which create one's births in saṃsāra and liberation to nirvāṇa.
27. The jñeyāvarana (shes.sgrib), the obscurations of the traces of conflicting emotions, the final veil to the knowledge of everything.
28. The Sanskrit word yāna, theg.pa in Tibetan, means something which supports goods on a journey. The journey in this context being the inner voyage to realization of our actual nature, covered by means to the "vehicle" of a specific spiritual tradition suited to our individual capacity and inclination.

༄། །རྫོགས་པ་ཆེན་པོ་ཀློང་ཆེན་སྙིང་ཐིག་གི་སྔོན་འགྲོའི་

ངག་འདོན་ཁྲིགས་སུ་བསྡེབས་པ་རྣམ་མཁྱེན་

ལམ་བཟང་ཞེས་བྱ་བ་བཞུགས་སོ།།

༄༅། གདོད་ནས་མངོན་སངས་རྒྱས་ཀྱང་གང་ལ་གང་འདུལ་གཟུགས་སྐུ་འགགས་པ་མེད།

སྣ་ཚོགས་སྤྲུ་འཕྲུལ་ངོམ་ཡང་ཕུང་ཁམས་སྐྱེ་མཆེད་གཟུང་དང་འཛིན་པ་བྲལ།

མི་ཡི་གཟུགས་སུ་སྣང་ཡང་མཁྱེན་བརྩེའི་འོད་ཟེར་སྟོང་འབར་རྒྱལ་བ་དངོས།

ཚེ་འདི་ཙམ་དུ་མ་ཡིན་གཏན་གྱི་སྐྱབས་སུ་ཁྱོད་བསྟེན་བྱིན་གྱིས་རློབས།།

དེ་ལ་འདིར་རྫོགས་པ་ཆེན་པོ་ཀློང་ཆེན་སྙིང་ཐིག་གི་སྔོན་དུ་འགྲོ་བའི་ངག་འདོན་ཁྲིགས་སུ་སྡེབས་པར།

དང་པོ་དཔལ་ལྡན་བླ་མའི་ཐུགས་རྒྱུད་བསྐུལ་ཕྱིར་གསོལ་བ་གདབ་པ་ནི།

༡ བླ་མ་མཁྱེན། (ལན་གསུམ། ཞེས་གདུང་བ་དྲག་པོས་པོས་ནས།)

༡ སྙིང་དབུས་དད་པའི་གེ་སར་བཞད་པ་ནས།

༢ སྐྱབས་གཅིག་དྲིན་ཅན་བླ་མ་ཡར་ལ་བཞེངས།

༣ ལས་དང་ཉོན་མོངས་དྲག་པོས་གཟིར་བ་ཡི།

༤ སྐལ་བ་ངན་པ་བདག་ལ་སྐྱོབ་པའི་ཕྱིར།

༥ སྤྱི་བོ་བདེ་ཆེན་འཁོར་ལོའི་རྒྱན་དུ་བཞུགས།

༦ དྲན་དང་ཤེས་བཞིན་ཀུན་ཀྱང་བཞེངས་སུ་གསོལ།

༡ ད་རེས་དམྱལ་བ་ཡི་དྭགས་དུད་འགྲོ་དང་།

༢ ཚེ་རིང་ལྷ་དང་ཀླ་ཀློ་ལོག་ལྟ་ཅན།

༣ སངས་རྒྱས་མ་བྱོན་ཞིང་དང་ལྐུགས་པ་སྟེ།

༤ མི་ཁོམ་བརྒྱད་ལས་ཐར་བའི་དལ་བ་ཐོབ།

༥ མིར་གྱུར་དབང་པོ་ཚང་དང་ཡུལ་དབུས་སྐྱེས།

༦ ལས་མཐའ་མ་ལོག་བསྟན་ལ་དད་པ་སྟེ།

༧ རང་ཉིད་འཁོར་བ་ལྷ་ཚང་སངས་རྒྱས་ཐོན།

༨ ཆོས་གསུངས་བསྟན་པ་གནས་དང་དེ་ལ་ཞུགས།

༩ བཤེས་གཉེན་དམ་པས་ཟིན་དང་གཞན་འཁོར་ལྔ།

༡༠ ཐམས་ཅད་རང་ལ་ཚང་བའི་གནས་ཐོབ་ཀྱང་།

༡༡ རྐྱེན་མང་ངེས་པ་མེད་པའི་ཆོས་སྤྱངས་ནས།

༡༢ འཇིག་རྟེན་ཕ་རོལ་ཉིད་དུ་སོན་པར་འགྱུར།

༡༣ བློ་སྣ་ཆོས་ལ་བསྒྱུར་ཅིག་གུ་རུ་མཁྱེན།

༡༤ ལམ་གོལ་དམན་པར་མ་གཏོང་ཀུན་མཁྱེན་རྗེ།

༡༥ གཉིས་སུ་མེད་དོ་དྲིན་ཅན་བླ་མ་མཁྱེན།

༡ ད་རེས་དལ་རྟེན་དོན་ཡོད་མ་བྱས་ན།

༢ ཕྱིས་ནས་ཐར་པ་བསྒྲུབ་པའི་རྟེན་མི་རྙེད།

༣ བདེ་འགྲོའི་རྟེན་ལ་བསོད་ནམས་ཟད་གྱུར་ནས།

༤ ཤི་བའི་འོག་ཏུ་ངན་སོང་ངན་འགྲོར་འཁྱམས།

༥ དགེ་སྡིག་མི་ཤེས་ཆོས་ཀྱི་སྒྲ་མི་ཐོས།

༦ དགེ་བའི་བཤེས་དང་མི་མཇལ་མཚང་རེ་ཆེ།

༧ སེམས་ཅན་ཙམ་གྱི་གྲངས་དང་རིམ་པ་ལ།

༨ བསམས་ན་མི་ལུས་ཐོབ་པ་སྲིད་མཐའ་ཙམ།

༩ མི་ཡང་ཆོས་མེད་སྡིག་ལ་སྤྱོད་མཐོང་ན།

༡༠ ཆོས་བཞིན་སྤྱོད་པ་ཉིན་མོའི་སྐར་མ་ཙམ།

༡༡ བློ་སྣ་ཆོས་ལ་བསྒྱུར་ཅིག་གུ་རུ་མཁྱེན།

༡༢ ལམ་གོལ་དམན་པར་མ་གཏོང་ཀུན་མཁྱེན་རྗེ།

༡༣ གཉིས་སུ་མེད་དོ་དྲིན་ཅན་བླ་མ་མཁྱེན།

༡ གལ་ཏེ་མི་ལུས་རིན་ཆེན་གླིང་ཕྱིན་ཡང་།

༢ ལུས་རྟེན་བཟང་ལ་བྱུར་པོ་ཆེ་ཡི་སེམས།

༣ ཐར་པ་བསྒྲུབ་པའི་རྟེན་དུ་མི་རུང་ཞིང་།

༤ ཁྱད་པར་བདུད་ཀྱིས་ཟིན་དང་དུག་ལྔ་འཁྲུགས།

༥ ལས་ངན་ཐོག་ཏུ་བབས་དང་ལེ་ལོས་གཡེངས།

༦ གཞན་ཁོལ་བྲན་གཡོག་འཛེགས་སྐྱིབ་ཆོས་ལྟར་བཅོས།

༧ སྨྱོངས་སོགས་འཕྲལ་བྱུང་རྐྱེན་གྱི་མི་ཁོམ་བརྒྱད།

༨ བདག་ལ་ཆོས་ཀྱི་འགལ་ཟླར་ལྷགས་པའི་ཚེ།

༩ བློ་སྣ་ཆོས་ལ་བསྒྱུར་ཅིག་གུ་རུ་མཁྱེན།

༡༠ ལམ་གོལ་དམན་པར་མ་གཏོང་ཀུན་མཁྱེན་རྗེ།

༡༡ གཉིས་སུ་མེད་དོ་དྲིན་ཅན་བླ་མ་མཁྱེན།

༡ སྐྱེ་ཤས་ཆུང་ཞིང་དད་པའི་ནོར་དང་བྲལ།

༢ འདོད་སྲེད་ཞགས་པས་བཅིངས་དང་ཀུན་སྤྱོད་རྩུབ།

༣ མི་དགེ་སྡིག་ལ་མི་འཛེམ་ལས་མཐའ་ལོག།

༤ སྡོམ་པ་ཉམས་ཤིང་དམ་ཚིག་རལ་བ་སྟེ།

༥ རིས་ཆད་བློ་ཡི་མི་ཁོམ་རྣམ་པ་བརྒྱད།

༦ བདག་ལ་ཆོས་ཀྱི་འགལ་ཟླར་ལྷགས་པའི་ཚེ།

༧ བློ་སྣ་ཚོགས་ལ་བསྒྱུར་ཅིག་གུ་རུ་མཁྱེན།
༨ ལམ་གོལ་དམན་པར་མ་གཏོང་ཀུན་མཁྱེན་རྗེ།
༩ གཉིས་སུ་མེད་དོ་དྲིན་ཅན་བླ་མ་མཁྱེན།

༡ ད་ལྟ་ནད་དང་སྡུག་བསྔལ་གྱིས་མ་གཟིར།
༢ བྲན་ཁོལ་ལ་སོགས་གཞན་དབང་མ་གྱུར་པས།
༣ རང་དབང་ཐོབ་པའི་རྟེན་འབྲེལ་འགྲིག་དུས་འདིར།
༤ སློམས་ལས་ངང་དུ་དལ་འབྱོར་ཆུད་གསོན་ན།
༥ འཁོར་དང་ལོངས་སྤྱོད་ཉེ་དུ་འབྲེལ་བ་ལྟ།
༦ ལྟ་ཅི་གཅེས་པར་བཟུང་བའི་ལུས་འདི་ཡང་།
༧ མལ་གྱི་ནང་ནས་ས་ཕྱོགས་སྟོང་པར་བསྐྱལ།
༨ ཕ་དང་བུ་གོད་ཁྱི་ཡིས་འདྲད་པའི་དུས།
༩ བར་དོའི་ཡུལ་ན་འཇིགས་པ་ཤིན་ཏུ་ཆེ།
༡༠ བློ་སྣ་ཚོགས་ལ་བསྒྱུར་ཅིག་གུ་རུ་མཁྱེན།
༡༡ ལམ་གོལ་དམན་པར་མ་གཏོང་ཀུན་མཁྱེན་རྗེ།
༡༢ གཉིས་སུ་མེད་དོ་དྲིན་ཅན་བླ་མ་མཁྱེན།

༡ དགེ་སྡིག་ལས་ཀྱི་རྣམ་སྨིན་ཕྱི་བཞིན་འབྲང་།

༡ ཁྱད་པར་དམྱལ་བའི་འཇིག་རྟེན་ཉིད་སོན་ན།
༢ ལྕགས་བསྲེགས་གཞིར་མཚོན་གྱིས་མགོ་ལུས་འདྲལ།
༣ སོག་ལེས་གསོག་དང་ཐོ་ལུམ་འབར་བས་འཚེར།

༤ སྣོ་མེད་ལྕུགས་ཁྲིམ་འཐུམས་པར་འོ་དོད་འབོད།

༥ འབར་བའི་གསལ་ཤིང་གིས་འབུགས་ཁྲོ་ཆུར་འཚོད།

༦ ཀུན་ནས་ཚ་བའི་མེས་བསྲེགས་བརྒྱད་ཚན་གཅིག།

༧ གངས་རི་སྦུག་པོའི་འདབས་དང་ཆུ་འཁྱགས་ཀྱི།

༨ གཅོང་རོང་ཡ་ངའི་གནས་སུ་བུ་ཡུག་སྦྲེབས།

༩ གྲང་རེག་རླུང་གིས་བཏབ་པའི་ལང་ཚོ་ནི།

༡༠ ཆུ་བུར་ཅན་དང་ལྷག་པར་བརྡོལ་བ་ཅན།

༡༡ སྨྲེ་སྔགས་རྒྱུན་མི་ཆད་པར་འདོན་པ་ཡང་།

༡༢ ཚོར་བའི་སྡུག་བསྔལ་བརྟག་པར་དཀའ་བ་ཡིས།

༡༣ ཟུངས་ཀྱིས་རབ་བཏང་འཆི་ཁའི་ནད་པ་བཞིན།

༡༤ ཤུགས་རིང་འདོན་ཅིང་སོ་ཐམ་པགས་པ་འགས།

༡༥ ཤའུ་ཐོན་ནས་ལྷག་པར་འགས་ཏེ་བརྒྱད།

༡༦ དེ་བཞིན་སྤྲུ་གྲིའི་ཐང་ལ་རྐང་པ་གཤོགས།

༡༧ རལ་གྲིའི་ཚལ་དུ་ལུས་ལ་བཅད་གཏུབས་བྱེད།

༡༨ རོ་རྨུགས་འདམ་ཚུད་ཐལ་ཚན་རབ་མེད་གླིང་།

༡༩ མནར་བའི་ཉེ་འཁོར་བ་དང་འགྱུར་བ་ཅན།

༢༠ སྣོ་དང་ཀ་བ་ཐབ་དང་ཐག་པ་སོགས།

༢༡ རྟག་ཏུ་བཀོལ་ཞིང་སྤྱོད་པའི་ཉེ་ཚེ་བ།

༢༢ རྣམ་གྲངས་བཅོ་བརྒྱད་གང་ལས་འབྱུང་བའི་རྒྱུ།

༢༣ ཞེ་སྡང་དྲག་པོའི་ཀུན་སློང་སྐྱེས་པའི་ཚེ།

༢༤ བློ་སྣ་ཆོས་ལ་བསྒྱུར་ཅིག་གུ་རུ་མཁྱེན།

༢༥ ལམ་གོལ་དམན་པར་མ་གཏོང་ཀུན་མཁྱེན་རྗེ།

༢༦ གཉིས་སུ་མེད་དོ་དྲིན་ཅན་བླ་མ་མཁྱེན།

༡ དེ་བཞིན་ཡོངས་ལ་ཉམས་མི་དགའ་བའི་ཡུལ།

༢ བཟའ་བཏུང་ལོངས་སྤྱོད་མིང་ཡང་མི་གྲགས་པར།

༣ ཟས་སྐོམ་ལོ་ཟླར་མི་རྙེད་ཡི་དྭགས་ལུས།

༤ རིད་ཅིང་ལྡང་པའི་སྟོབས་ཉམས་ཇམ་པ་གསུམ།

༥ གང་ལས་འབྱུང་བའི་རྒྱུ་ནི་སེར་སྣ་ཡིན།

༦ གཅིག་ལ་གཅིག་ཟ་གསོད་པའི་འཇིག་པ་ཆེ།

༧ བཀོལ་ཞིང་སྤྱོད་པས་ཉམ་ཐག་བླང་དོར་རྨོངས།

༨ ཕ་མཐའ་མེད་པའི་སྡུག་བསྔལ་གྱིས་གཟིར་བའི།

༩ ས་བོན་གཏི་མུག་མུན་པར་འཁྱམས་པ་བདག།

༡༠ བློ་སྣ་ཆོས་ལ་བསྒྱུར་ཅིག་གུ་རུ་མཁྱེན།

༡༡ ལམ་གོལ་དམན་པར་མ་གཏོང་ཀུན་མཁྱེན་རྗེ།

༡༢ གཉིས་སུ་མེད་དོ་དྲིན་ཅན་བླ་མ་མཁྱེན།

༡ ཆོས་ལམ་ཞུགས་ཀྱང་ཉེས་སྤྱོད་མི་སྡོམ་ཞིང་།

༢ ཐེག་ཆེན་སྒོར་ཞུགས་གཞན་ཕན་སེམས་དང་བྲལ།

༣ དབང་བཞི་ཐོབ་ཀྱང་བསྐྱེད་རྫོགས་མི་སྒོམ་པའི།

༤ ལམ་གོལ་འདི་ལས་བླ་མས་བསྒྲལ་དུ་གསོལ།

༥ ལྟ་བ་མ་རྟོགས་ཐོ་ཅོའི་སྤྱོད་པ་ཅན།

༦ སྒོམ་པ་ཡེངས་ཀྱང་གོ་ཡུལ་ཟུད་གོག་འཐག།

༧ སྤྱོད་པ་ནོར་ཀྱང་རང་སྐྱོན་མི་སེམས་པའི།

༨ ཆོས་ཉིད་འདི་ལས་བླ་མས་བསྒྲལ་དུ་གསོལ།

༩ ནངས་པར་འཆི་ཡང་གནས་གོས་ནོར་ལ་སྲེད།

༡༠ ན་ཚོད་ཡོལ་ཡང་ངེས་འབྱུང་སྐྱོ་ཤས་བྲལ།

༡༡ ཐོས་པ་ཆུང་ཡང་ཡོན་ཏན་ཅན་དུ་རློམ།

༡༢ མ་རིག་འདི་ལས་བླ་མས་བསྒྲལ་དུ་གསོལ།

༡༣ རྐྱེན་ཁར་འཚོར་ཡང་འདུ་འཛི་གནས་སྐོར་སེམས།

༡༤ དབེན་པར་བརྟེན་ཀྱང་རང་རྒྱུད་ཤིང་ལྟར་རེངས།

༡༥ དུལ་བར་སྨྲ་ཡང་ཆགས་སྡང་མ་ཞིག་པའི།

༡༦ ཆོས་བརྒྱད་འདི་ལས་བླ་མས་བསྒྲལ་དུ་གསོལ།

༡༧ གཉིད་འཐུག་འདི་ལས་མྱུར་དུ་སད་དུ་གསོལ།

༡༨ ཁྲིམས་མྱུན་འདི་ལས་མྱུར་དུ་དབྱུང་དུ་གསོལ།།

(ཞེས་འབོད་པ་དྲག་པོས་ཐུགས་རྗེ་ཀློངས་པར་བྱའོ།།)

གཉིས་པ་སྐྱབས་སུ་འགྲོ་བ་ནི།

༡ དཀོན་མཆོག་གསུམ་དངོས་བདེ་གཤེགས་རྩ་བ་གསུམ༔

༢ རྩ་རླུང་ཐིག་ལེའི་རང་བཞིན་བྱང་ཆུབ་སེམས༔

༣ ངོ་བོ་རང་བཞིན་ཐུགས་རྗེའི་དཀྱིལ་འཁོར་ལ༔

༤ བྱང་ཆུབ་སྙིང་པོའི་བར་དུ་སྐྱབས་སུ་མཆི༔ (ལན་གསུམ༔)

གསུམ་པ་སེམས་བསྐྱེད་ནི།

༡ ཧོཿ་ སྣ་ཚོགས་སྣང་བ་ཆུ་ཟླའི་རྫུན་རིས་ཀྱི༔

༢ འཁོར་བ་ལུ་གུ་རྒྱུད་དུ་འཁྱམས་པའི་འགྲོ༔

༣ རང་རིག་འོད་གསལ་དབྱིངས་སུ་ངལ་གསོའི་ཕྱིར༔

༤ ཚད་མེད་བཞི་ཡི་ངང་ནས་སེམས་བསྐྱེད་དོ༔ (ལན་གསུམ༔)

བཞི་པ་རྡོར་སེམས་བསྒོམ་བཟླས་ནི།

༡ ཨཱཿ་ བདག་ཉིད་ཐ་མལ་སྤྱི་བོ་རུ༔

༢ པད་དཀར་ཟླ་བའི་གདན་གྱི་དབུས༔

༣ ཧཱུྃ་ལས་བླ་མ་རྡོ་རྗེ་སེམས༔

༤ དཀར་གསལ་ལོངས་སྤྱོད་རྫོགས་པའི་སྐུ༔

༥ རྡོ་རྗེ་དྲིལ་འཛིན་སྙེམས་མ་འཁྲིལ༔

༦ ཁྱོད་ལ་སྐྱབས་གསོལ་སྡིག་པ་སྦྱོང༔

༧ འགྱོད་སེམས་དྲག་པོས་མཐོལ་ལོ་བཤགས༔

༨ ཕྱིན་ཆད་སྲོག་ལ་བབ་ཀྱང་སྡོམ༔

༩ ཁྱོད་ཐུགས་ཟླ་བ་རྒྱས་པའི་སྟེང༔

༡༠ ཧཱུྃ་ཡིག་མཐའ་མར་སྔགས་ཀྱིས་བསྐོར༔

༡༡ བཟླས་པ་སྔགས་ཀྱིས་རྒྱུད་བསྐུལ་བས༔

༡༢ ཡབ་ཡུམ་བདེ་རོལ་སྦྱོར་མཚམས་ནས༔

༡༣ བདུད་རྩི་བྱང་ཆུབ་སེམས་ཀྱི་སྤྲིན༔

༡༤ ག་བུར་རྡུལ་ལྟར་འཛག་པ་ཡིས༔

༡༥ བདག་དང་ཁམས་གསུམ་སེམས་ཅན་གྱི༔

༡༦ ལས་དང་ཉོན་མོངས་སྡུག་བསྔལ་རྒྱུ༔

༡༧ ནད་གདོན་སྡིག་སྒྲིབ་ཉེས་ལྟུང་གྲིབ༔

༡༨ མ་ལུས་བྱང་བར་མཛད་དུ་གསོལ༔

༡ ཨོཾ་བཛྲ་སཏྭ་ས་མ་ཡ༔

༢ མ་ནུ་པཱ་ལ་ཡ༔

༣ བཛྲ་སཏྭ་ཏེ་ནོ་པ༔

༤ ཏིཥྛ་དྲྀ་ཌྷོ་མེ་བྷ་ཝ༔

༥ སུ་ཏོཥྱོ་མེ་བྷ་ཝ༔

༦ སུ་པོཥྱོ་མེ་བྷ་ཝ༔

༧ ཨ་ནུ་རཀྟོ་མེ་བྷ་ཝ༔

༨ སརྦ་སིདྡྷི་མྨེ་པྲ་ཡཙྪ༔

༩ སརྦ་ཀརྨ་སུ་ཙ་མེ༔

༡༠ ཙིཏྟཾ་ཤྲེ་ཡཾ༔ཀུ་རུ་ཧཱུྃ༔

༡༡ ཧ་ཧ་ཧ་ཧ་ཧོ༔

༡༢ བྷ་ག་ཝཱན་སརྦ་ཏ་ཐཱ་ག་ཏ་བཛྲ་མཱ་མེ་མུཉྩ༔

༡༣ བཛྲཱི་བྷ་ཝ་མ་ཧཱ་ས་མ་ཡ་ས་ཏྭ་ཨཱ༔ (ཞེས་ཡི་གེ་བརྒྱ་པ་ཅི་ནུས་བཟླས་མཐར།)

༡ མགོན་པོ་བདག་ནི་མི་ཤེས་རྨོངས་པ་ཡིས༔

༢ དམ་ཚིག་ལས་ནི་འགལ་ཞིང་ཉམས༔

༣ བླ་མ་མགོན་པོས་སྐྱབས་མཛོད་ཅིག༔

༤ གཙོ་བོ་རྡོ་རྗེ་འཛིན་པ་སྟེ།

༥ ཐུགས་རྗེ་ཆེན་པོའི་བདག་ཉིད་ཅན༔

༦ འགྲོ་བའི་གཙོ་ལ་བདག་སྐྱབས་མཆི༔

༡ སྐུ་གསུང་ཐུགས་རྩ་བ་དང་ཡན་ལག་གི་དམ་ཚིག་ཉམས་པ་ཐམས་ཅད་མཐོལ་ལོ་བཤགས་སོ༔

༢ སྡིག་པ་དང་སྒྲིབ་པ་ཉེས་ལྟུང་དྲི་མའི་ཚོགས་ཐམས་ཅད་བྱང་ཞིང་དག་པར་མཛད་དུ་གསོལ༔

༣ ཅེས་བརྗོད་པས་རྡོ་རྗེ་སེམས་དཔའ་དགྱེས་བཞིན་འཛུམ་པ་དང་བཅས་པས་རིགས་ཀྱི་བུ་ཁྱོད་ཀྱི་སྡིག་སྒྲིབ་ཉེས་ལྟུང་ཐམས་ཅད་དག་པ་ཡིན་ནོ། ཞེས་གནང་བ་བྱིན་ཞིང་། འོད་དུ་ཞུ་ནས་རང་ལ་ཐིམ་པའི་རྐྱེན་ལས།

༤ རང་ཉིད་ཀྱང་རྡོ་རྗེ་སེམས་དཔའ་སྣང་སྟོང་མེ་ལོང་ནང་གི་གཟུགས་བརྙན་ལྟ་བུར་གྱུར་པའི་ཐུགས་སྲོག་ཧཱུྃ་གི་མཐའ་མར་ཡི་གེར་འབྲུ་བཞི་པོ་གསལ་བ་ལས་འོད་ཟེར་འཕྲོས་ཁམས་གསུམ་སྣོད་བཅུད་དང་བཅས་པ་རྡོར་སེམས་རིགས་ལྔའི་རྟེན་དང་བརྟེན་པའི་རང་བཞིན་དུ་སངས་རྒྱས་པར་བསམས་ལ།

༥ ཨོཾ་བཛྲ་སཏྭ་ཧཱུྃ༔ (ཅི་ནུས་བཟླས་མཐར་མཉམ་པར་བཞག་གོ།)

ལྔ་པ་མཇལ་ནི།

༡ ཨོཾ་ཨཱཿཧཱུྃ། སྟོང་གསུམ་འཛིག་རྟེན་བྱེ་བ་ཕྲག་བརྒྱའི་ཞིང༔

༢ རིན་ཆེན་སྣ་བདུན་ལྷ་མིའི་འབྱོར་པས་གཏམས༔

༣ བདག་ལུས་ལོངས་སྤྱོད་བཅས་པ་ཡོངས་འབུལ་གྱིས༔

༤ ཆོས་ཀྱི་འཁོར་ལོས་བསྒྱུར་བའི་སྲིད་ཐོབ་ཤོག༔

༡ འོག་མིན་བདེ་ཆེན་སྟུག་པོ་བཀོད་པའི་ཞིང༔

༢ ངེས་པ་ལྔ་ལྡན་རིགས་ལྔའི་ཚོམ་བུ་ཅན༔

༣ འདོད་ཡོན་མཆོད་པའི་སྤྲིན་ཕུང་བསམ་ཡས་པ༔

༤ ཕུལ་བས་ལོངས་སྐུའི་ཞིང་ལ་སྤྱོད་པར་ཤོག༔

༡ སྣང་སྲིད་རྣམ་དག་གཞོན་ནུ་བུམ་པའི་སྐུ༔

༢ ཐུགས་རྗེ་མ་འགགས་ཆོས་ཉིད་རོལ་པས་བརྒྱན༔

༣ སྐུ་དང་ཐིག་ལེའི་འཛིན་པ་རྣམ་དག་ཞིང༔

༤ ཕུལ་བས་ཆོས་སྐུའི་ཞིང་ལ་སྤྱོད་པར་ཤོག༔

དྲུག་པ་ཀུ་སུ་ལུའི་ཚོགས་གསོག་ནི༔

༡ ཕཊ༔ ལུས་གཅེས་འཛིན་བོར་བས་ལྷ་བདུད་ཆོམ༔

༢ སེམས་ཚངས་པའི་སྒོ་ནས་དབྱིངས་ལ་ཐོན༔

༣ འཆི་བདག་གི་བདུད་བཅོམ་ཁྲོས་མར་གྱུར༔

༤ གཡས་ཉོན་མོངས་བདུད་འཇོམས་གྲི་གུག་གིས༔

༥ གཟུགས་ཕུང་པོའི་བདུད་བཅོམ་ཐོད་པ་བྲེགས༔

༦ གཡོན་ལས་བྱེད་ཚུལ་གྱིས་བྷནྡྷ་ཐོགས༔

༧ སྐུ་གསུམ་གྱི་མི་མགོའི་སྒྱེད་པུར་བཞག༔

༨ ནང་སྟོང་གསུམ་གང་བའི་བམ་རོ་དེ༔

༩ ཨཱཿཐུང་དང་ཧཾ་ཡིག་གིས་བདུད་རྩིར་བཞུ༔
༡༠ འབྲུ་གསུམ་གྱི་ནུས་པས་སྦྱང་སྤེལ་བསྒྱུར༔

༡ ཨོཾ་ཨཱཿཧཱུྃ། (ཅི་ནུས་བཟླས་མཐར།)

༡ ཕཊ༔ ཡར་མཆོད་ཡུལ་མགྲོན་གྱི་ཐུགས་དམ་བསྐང༔
༢ ཚོགས་རྫོགས་ནས་མཆོད་ཐུན་དངོས་གྲུབ་ཐོབ༔
༣ མར་འཁོར་བའི་མགྲོན་མཉེས་ལན་ཆགས་བྱང༔
༤ ཁྱད་པར་གནོད་བྱེད་བགེགས་རིགས་ཚིམ༔
༥ ནད་གདོན་དང་བར་ཆད་དབྱིངས་སུ་ཞི༔
༦ རྐྱེན་ངན་དང་བདག་འཛིན་རྡུལ་དུ་བརླགས༔
༧ མཐར་མཆོད་བྱ་དང་མཆོད་བྱེད་མཆོད་ཡུལ་ཀུན༔
༨ གཤིས་རྫོགས་པ་ཆེན་པོར་མ་བཅོས་ཨཱཿ

བདུན་པ་བླ་མའི་རྣལ་འབྱོར་ནི།

༡ ཨེ་མ་ཧོ༔ རང་སྣང་ལྷུན་གྲུབ་དག་པ་རབ་འབྱམས་ཞིང༔
༢ བཀོད་པ་རབ་རྫོགས་ཟངས་མདོག་དཔལ་རིའི་དབུས༔
༣ རང་ཉིད་གཞི་ལུས་རྡོ་རྗེ་རྣལ་འབྱོར་མ༔
༤ ཞལ་གཅིག་ཕྱག་གཉིས་དམར་གསལ་གྲི་ཐོད་འཛིན༔
༥ ཞབས་གཉིས་རོལ་སྟབས་སྤྱན་གསུམ་ནམ་མཁར་གཟིགས༔
༦ སྤྱི་བོར་པདྨ་འབུམ་བརྡལ་ཉི་ཟླའི་སྟེང༔
༧ སྐྱབས་གནས་ཀུན་འདུས་རྩ་བའི་བླ་མ་དང༔

༨ དབྱེར་མེད་མཚོ་སྐྱེས་རྡོ་རྗེ་སྤྲུལ་པའི་སྐུ༔
༩ དཀར་དམར་མདངས་ལྡན་གཞོན་ནུའི་ཤ་ཚུགས་ཅན༔
༡༠ ཕོད་ཁ་ཆོས་གོས་ཟ་བེར་འདུང་མ་གསོལ༔
༡༡ ཞལ་གཅིག་ཕྱག་གཉིས་རྒྱལ་པོ་རོལ་པའི་སྟབས༔
༡༢ ཕྱག་གཡས་རྡོ་རྗེ་གཡོན་པས་ཐོད་བུམ་བསྣམས༔
༡༣ དབུ་ལ་འདབ་ལྡན་པདྨའི་མཉེན་ཞུ་གསོལ༔
༡༤ མཆན་ཁུང་གཡོན་ན་བདེ་སྟོང་ཡུམ་མཆོག་མ༔
༡༥ སྦས་པའི་ཚུལ་གྱིས་ཁ་ཊཾ་ག་གསུམ་བསྣམས༔
༡༦ འཇའ་ཟེར་ཐིག་ལེའི་འོད་ཕུང་ཀློང་ན་བཞུགས༔
༡༧ ཕྱི་འཁོར་འོད་ལྔའི་དྭ་བས་མཛེས་པའི་ཀློང༔
༡༨ སྤྲུལ་པའི་རྗེ་འབངས་ཉི་ཤུ་རྩ་ལྔ་དང༔
༡༩ རྒྱ་བོད་པཎ་གྲུབ་རིག་འཛིན་ཡི་དམ་ལྷ༔
༢༠ མཁའ་འགྲོ་ཆོས་སྐྱོང་དམ་ཅན་སྤྲིན་ལྟར་གཏིབས༔
༢༡ གསལ་སྟོང་མཉམ་གནས་ཆེན་པོའི་ངང་དུ་གསལ༔

༡ ཧཱུྃ། ཨོ་རྒྱན་ཡུལ་གྱི་ནུབ་བྱང་མཚམས༔
༢ པདྨ་གེ་སར་སྡོང་པོ་ལ།
༣ ཡ་མཚན་མཆོག་གི་དངོས་གྲུབ་བརྙེས༔
༤ པདྨ་འབྱུང་གནས་ཞེས་སུ་གྲགས༔
༥ འཁོར་དུ་མཁའ་འགྲོ་མང་པོས་བསྐོར༔
༦ ཁྱེད་ཀྱི་རྗེས་སུ་བདག་བསྒྲུབ་ཀྱིས༔

༧ བྱིན་གྱིས་བརླབ་ཕྱིར་གཤེགས་སུ་གསོལ༔

༨ གུ་རུ་པདྨ་སིདྡྷི་ཧཱུྃ༔

༡ ཧྲཱི༔ བདག་ལུས་ཞིང་གི་རྡུལ་སྙེད་དུ༔

༢ རྣམ་པར་འཕྲུལ་པས་ཕྱག་འཚལ་ལོ༔

༣ དངོས་བཤམས་ཡིད་སྤྲུལ་ཏིང་འཛིན་མཐུས༔

༤ སྣང་སྲིད་མཆོད་པའི་ཕྱག་རྒྱར་འབུལ༔

༥ སྒོ་གསུམ་མི་དགེའི་ལས་རྣམས་ཀུན༔

༦ འོད་གསལ་ཆོས་སྐུའི་ངང་དུ་བཤགས༔

༧ བདེན་པ་གཉིས་ཀྱིས་བསྡུས་པ་ཡི༔

༨ དགེ་ཚོགས་ཀུན་ལ་རྗེས་ཡི་རང༔

༩ ཐེག་གསུམ་ཆོས་འཁོར་བསྐོར་བར་བསྐུལ༔

༡༠ ཇི་སྲིད་འཁོར་བ་མ་སྟོངས་བར༔

༡༡ མྱ་ངན་མི་འདའ་བཞུགས་གསོལ་འདེབས༔

༡༢ དུས་གསུམ་བསགས་པའི་དགེ་རྩ་ཀུན༔

༡༣ བྱང་ཆུབ་ཆེན་པོའི་རྒྱུ་རུ་བསྔོ༔

༡ རྗེ་བཙུན་གུ་རུ་རིན་པོ་ཆེ༔

༢ ཁྱེད་ནི་སངས་རྒྱས་ཐམས་ཅད་ཀྱི༔

༣ ཐུགས་རྗེ་བྱིན་རླབས་འདུས་པའི་དཔལ༔

༤ སེམས་ཅན་ཡོངས་ཀྱི་མགོན་གཅིག་པུ༔

༥ ལུས་དང་ལོངས་སྤྱོད་བློ་སྙིང་བྲང༔

༦ བློས་པ་མེད་པར་ཁྱེད་ལ་འབུལ༔
༧ འདི་ནས་བྱང་ཆུབ་མ་ཐོབ་པར༔
༨ སྐྱིད་སྡུག་ལེགས་ཉེས་མཐོ་དམན་ཀུན༔
༩ རྗེ་བཙུན་ཆེན་པོ་པད་འབྱུང་མཁྱེན༔

༡ བདག་ལ་རེ་ས་གཞན་ན་མེད༔
༢ ད་ལྟའི་དུས་ངན་སྙིགས་མའི་འགྲོ༔
༣ མི་བཟོད་སྡུག་བསྔལ་འདམ་དུ་བྱིངས༔
༤ འདི་ལས་སྐྱོབས་ཤིག་མ་ཧཱ་གུ་རུ༔
༥ དབང་བཞི་བསྐུར་ཅིག་བྱིན་རླབས་ཅན༔
༦ རྟོགས་པ་སྤྲོར་ཅིག་ཐུགས་རྗེ་ཅན༔
༧ སྒྲིབ་གཉིས་སྦྱོང་ཤིག་ནུས་མཐུ་ཅན༔

༡ ནམ་ཞིག་ཚེ་ཡི་དུས་བྱས་ཚེ༔
༢ རང་སྣང་ཟ་ཡབ་དཔལ་རིའི་ཞིང༔
༣ ཟུང་འཇུག་སྤྲུལ་པའི་ཞིང་ཁམས་སུ༔
༤ གཞི་ལུས་རྡོ་རྗེ་རྣལ་འབྱོར་མ༔
༥ གསལ་འཚེར་འོད་ཀྱི་གོང་བུ་རུ༔
༦ གྱུར་ནས་རྗེ་བཙུན་པད་འབྱུང་དང༔
༧ དབྱེར་མེད་ཆེན་པོར་སངས་རྒྱས་ཏེ༔
༨ བདེ་དང་སྟོང་པའི་ཆོ་འཕྲུལ་གྱིས༔
༩ ཡེ་ཤེས་ཆེན་པོའི་རོལ་པ་ལས༔

༡༠ ཁམས་གསུམ་སེམས་ཅན་མ་ལུས་པ༔

༡༡ འདྲེན་པའི་དེད་དཔོན་དམ་པ་རུ༔

༡༢ རྗེ་བཙུན་པདྨ་དབུགས་དབྱུང་གསོལ༔

༡༣ གསོལ་བ་སྙིང་གི་དཀྱིལ་ནས་འདེབས༔

༡༤ ཁ་ཙམ་ཚིག་ཙམ་མ་ཡིན་ནོ༔

༡༥ བྱིན་རླབས་ཐུགས་ཀྱི་ཀློང་ནས་སྩོལ༔

༡༦ བསམ་དོན་འགྲུབ་པར་མཛད་དུ་གསོལ༔

༡ ཨོཾ་ཨཱཿཧཱུྃ་བཛྲ་གུ་རུ་པདྨ་སིདྡྷི་ཧཱུྃ༔

བརྒྱུད་པ་བརྒྱུད་པའི་གསོལ་འདེབས་ནི།

༡ ཨེ་མ་ཧོ༔རྒྱ་ཆད་ཕྱོགས་ལྷུང་བྲལ་བའི་ཞིང་ཁམས་ནས༔

༢ དང་པོའི་སངས་རྒྱས་ཆོས་སྐུ་ཀུན་ཏུ་བཟང༔

༣ ལོངས་སྐུ་ཆུ་ཟླའི་རོལ་རྩལ་རྡོ་རྗེ་སེམས༔

༤ སྤྲུལ་སྐུར་མཚན་རྫོགས་དགའ་རབ་རྡོ་རྗེ་ལ༔

༥ གསོལ་བ་འདེབས་སོ་བྱིན་རླབས་དབང་བསྐུར་སྩོལ༔

༡ ཤྲཱི་སིཧྨ་དོན་དམ་ཆོས་ཀྱི་མཛོད༔

༢ འཇམ་དཔལ་བཤེས་གཉེན་ཐེག་དགུའི་འཁོར་ལོས་བསྒྱུར༔

༣ ཛྙཱ་ན་སཱུ་ཏྲ་པཎ་ཆེན་བི་མ་ལར༔

༤ གསོལ་འདེབས་སོ་གྲོལ་བྱེད་ལམ་སྣ་སྟོན༔

༡ འཛམ་བུ་གླིང་གི་རྒྱན་གཅིག་པདྨ་འབྱུང༔
༢ ငེས་པར་ཐུགས་ཀྱི་སྲས་མཆོག་རྗེ་འབངས་གྲོགས༔
༣ ཐུགས་གཏེར་རྒྱ་མཚོའི་བདྡ་གྲོལ་གླིང་ཆེན་ཞབས༔
༤ མཁའ་འགྲོའི་དབྱིངས་མཛོད་བཀའ་བབས་འཇིགས་མེད་གླིང༔
༥ གསོལ་བ་འདེབས་སོ་འབྲས་བུ་ཐོབ་གྲོལ་སྩོལ༔

བརྒྱུད་འདེབས་ཁ་སྐོང་།

༡ མཁས་ཤིང་གྲུབ་བརྙེས་ཀུན་བཟང་གཞན་ཕན་དཔལ།
༢ ཕྱག་ན་པདྨ་རྒྱལ་བའི་མྱུ་གུ་དང་།
༣ འཇམ་པའི་དབྱངས་དངོས་མཁན་ཆེན་པདྨའི་མཚན།
༤ གསོལ་བ་འདེབས་སོ་གནས་ལུགས་རང་ཞལ་སྟོན།

༡ ཁྱད་པར་ཟབ་མོ་འོད་གསལ་སྙིང་ཐིག་གི།
༢ ཤིང་རྟ་ཆེན་པོ་མདོ་སྔགས་གླིང་པའི་ཞབས།
༣ བཀའ་དྲིན་མཉམ་མེད་རྩ་བའི་བླ་མ་ལ།
༤ གསོལ་བ་འདེབས་སོ་དོན་གཉིས་ལྷུན་གྲུབ་མཛོད།

༡ སྲིད་ལས་ངེས་པར་འབྱུང་བའི་ཞེན་ལོག་གིས༔
༢ དོ་རྗེའི་བླ་མ་དོན་ལྡན་མིག་བཞིན་བསྟེན༔
༣ ཅི་གསུང་བཀའ་བསྒྲུབ་ཟབ་མོའི་ཉམས་ལེན་ལ༔
༤ ལྷེམ་རྒྱང་མེད་པའི་སྒྲུབ་ཚུགས་ཞེ་རུས་ཀྱིས༔
༥ ཐུགས་རྒྱུད་དགོངས་པའི་བྱིན་རླབས་འཕོ་བར་ཤོག༔

༦ སྣང་སྲིད་འདས་ཡེ་ནས་འོག་མིན་ཞིང༔

༧ ལྷ་སྔགས་ཆོས་སྐུར་དག་རྫོགས་སྨིན་པའི་འབྲས༔

༨ སྤང་བླང་བྱ་རྩོལ་མེད་པའི་རྫོགས་པ་ཆེ༔

༩ ཤེས་ཉམས་ཡིད་དཔྱོད་ལས་འདས་རིག་པའི་གདངས༔

༡༠ ཆོས་ཉིད་མངོན་སུམ་ཧེ་ནན་པར་མཐོང་བར་ཤོག༔

༡༡ མཚན་མའི་རྟོག་པ་རྣམ་གྲོལ་འཇའ་ཟེར་སྦྲུབས༔

༡༢ སྐུ་དང་ཐིག་ལེའི་ཉམས་སྣང་གོང་དུ་འཕེལ༔

༡༣ རིག་རྩལ་ལོངས་སྐུའི་ཞིང་ཁམས་ཚད་ལ་ཕེབས༔

༡༤ ཆོས་ཟད་བློ་འདས་ཆེན་པོར་སངས་རྒྱས་ཏེ༔

༡༥ གཞོན་ནུ་བུམ་སྐུར་གཏན་སྲིད་ཟིན་པར་ཤོག༔

༡ ཤིན་ཏུ་རྣལ་འབྱོར་ཉམས་འོག་མ་ཆུད་དེ༔

༢ རགས་ལུས་དྭངས་མའི་དབྱིངས་སུ་མ་གྲོལ་ན༔

༣ ནམ་ཞིག་ཚེ་ཡི་འདུ་བྱེད་བསྡུང་བའི་ཚེ༔

༤ འཆི་བ་འོད་གསལ་ཀ་དག་ཆོས་སྐུར་ཤར༔

༥ བར་དོའི་སྣང་ཆ་ལོངས་སྤྱོད་རྫོགས་སྐུར་གྲོལ༔

༦ ཁྲེགས་ཆོད་ཐོད་རྒལ་ལམ་གྱི་རྩལ་རྫོགས་ནས༔

༧ མ་པང་བུ་འཛུག་ལྷ་བུར་གྲོལ་བར་ཤོག༔

༡ གསང་ཆེན་འོད་གསལ་ཐེག་པ་མཆོག་གི་རྩེ༔

༢ སངས་རྒྱས་གཞན་ནས་མི་འཚོལ་ཆོས་སྐུའི་ཞལ༔

༣ མངོན་གྱུར་གདོད་མའི་ས་ལ་མ་གྲོལ་ན༔

༤ མ་སྨོམ་སངས་རྒྱས་ཆོས་ལྡིའི་ལམ་མཆོག་ལ༔

༥ བརྟེན་ནས་རང་བཞིན་སྤྲུལ་པའི་ཞིང་ལྡི་དང༔

༦ ཁྲིད་པར་པདྨ་འོད་ཀྱི་ཕོ་བྲང་དུ༔

༧ རིག་འཛིན་རྒྱ་མཚོའི་གཙོ་མཆོག་ཨོ་རྒྱན་རྗེས༔

༨ གསང་ཆེན་ཆོས་ཀྱི་དགའ་སྟོན་འགྱེད་པའི་སར༔

༩ སྲས་ཀྱི་ཐུ་བོར་སྐྱེས་ནས་དབུགས་དབྱུང་སྟེ༔

༡༠ མཐའ་ཡས་འགྲོ་བའི་ཉེར་འཚོར་བདག་འགྱུར་ཤོག༔

༡ རིག་འཛིན་རྒྱལ་བ་རྒྱ་མཚོའི་བྱིན་རླབས་དང༔

༢ ཆོས་དབྱིངས་བསམ་མི་ཁྱབ་པའི་བདེན་པ་ཡིས༔

༣ དལ་འབྱོར་རྟེན་ལ་རྫོགས་སྨིན་སྦྱངས་གསུམ་གྱི༔

༤ རྟེན་འབྲེལ་མངོན་གྱུར་སངས་རྒྱས་ཐོབ་པར་ཤོག༔

(ཅེས་ཁ་ཞེ་མེད་པར་གསོལ་བ་སྙིང་ནས་གདབ་བོ༔)

དགུ་པ་དབང་བཞི་བླངས་པ་ནི།

༡ གུ་རུའི་སྨིན་མཚམས་ནས་ཨོཾ་ཡིག་ཆུ་ཤེལ་ལྟ་བུར་འཚེར་བ་ལས་འོད་ཟེར་འཕྲོས༔

༢ རང་གི་སྤྱི་བ་ནས་ཞུགས༔

༣ ལུས་ཀྱི་ལས་དང་རྩའི་སྒྲིབ་པ་དག༔

༤ སྐུ་རྡོ་རྗེའི་བྱིན་རླབས་ཞུགས༔

༥ བུམ་པའི་དབང་ཐོབ།

༦ བསྐྱེད་རིམ་གྱི་སྣོད་དུ་གྱུར།

༧ རྣམ་སྨིན་རིག་འཛིན་གྱི་ས་བོན་ཐེབས༔

༨ སྤྲུལ་སྐུའི་གོ་འཕང་ཐོབ་པའི་སྐལ་བ་རྒྱུད་ལ་བཞག༔

༡ མཁྱེན་པ་ནས་ཨཱཿཡིག་པདྨ་རཱ་ག་ལྟར་འབར་བ་ལས་འོད་ཟེར་འཕྲོས༔

༢ རང་གི་མཁྱེན་པ་ནས་ཞུགས།

༣ ངག་གི་ལས་དང་རླུང་གི་སྒྲིབ་པ་དག༔

༤ གསུང་རྡོ་རྗེའི་བྱིན་རླབས་ཞུགས༔

༥ གསང་བའི་དབང་ཐོབ།

༦ བཟླས་བརྗོད་ཀྱི་སྣོད་དུ་གྱུར༔

༧ ཚེ་དབང་རིག་འཛིན་གྱི་ས་བོན་ཐེབས༔

༨ ལོངས་སྤྱོད་རྫོགས་པའི་གོ་འཕང་གི་སྐལ་བ་རྒྱུད་ལ་བཞག༔

༡ ཐུགས་ཀའི་ཧཱུྃ་ཡིག་ནམ་མཁའི་མདོག་ཅན་ལས་འོད་ཟེར་འཕྲོས༔

༢ རང་གི་སྙིང་ག་ནས་ཞུགས།

༣ ཡིད་ཀྱི་ལས་དང་ཐིག་ལེའི་སྒྲིབ་པ་དག༔

༤ ཐུགས་རྡོ་རྗེའི་བྱིན་རླབས་ཞུགས༔

༥ ཤེས་རབ་ཡེ་ཤེས་ཀྱི་དབང་ཐོབ༔

༦ བདེ་སྟོང་ཙཎྜ་ལིའི་སྣོད་དུ་གྱུར༔

༧ ཕྱག་རྒྱའི་རིག་འཛིན་གྱི་ས་བོན་ཐེབས༔

༨ ཆོས་སྐུའི་གོ་འཕང་ཐོབ་པའི་སྐལ་བ་རྒྱུད་ལ་བཞག༔

༡ སྣར་ཡང་ཐུགས་ཀའི་ཧཱུྃ་ལས་ཧཱུྃ་ཡིག་གཉིས་པ་ཞིག་སྐར་མདའ་འཕངས་པ་
བཞིན་དུ་ཆད༔

༢ རང་སེམས་དང་ཐ་དད་མེད་པར་འདྲེས༔

༣ ཀུན་གཞིའི་ལས་དང་ཤེས་བྱའི་སྒྲིབ་པ་སྦྱངས༔

༤ ཡེ་ཤེས་རྡོ་རྗེའི་བྱིན་རླབས་ཞུགས།

༥ ཚིག་གིས་མཚོན་པ་དོན་དམ་གྱི་དབང་ཐོབ༔

༦ ཀ་དག་རྫོགས་པ་ཆེན་པོའི་སྣོད་དུ་གྱུར༔

༧ ལྷུན་གྲུབ་རིག་འཛིན་གྱི་ས་བོན་ཐེབས༔

༨ མཐར་ཐུག་གི་འབྲས་བུ་ངོ་བོ་ཉིད་སྐུའི་སྐལ་བ་རྒྱུད་ལ་བཞག༔

(དེ་ལྟར་འདོན་བསྒོམ་ཟུང་འཇུག་པས་ལམ་དབང་བླངས་མཐར།)

༡ བླ་མའི་ཐུགས་ཀ་ནས་འོད་ཟེར་དམར་པོ་དྲོད་དང་བཅས་པ་ཞིག་ཤལ་གྱིས་
བྱུང་བ་བདག་ཉིད་རྡོ་རྗེ་རྣལ་འབྱོར་མར་གསལ་བའི་སྙིང་ཁར་རེག་པ་ཙམ་
གྱིས་འོད་དམར་གྱི་གོང་བུ་ཞིག་ཏུ་གྱུར་ནས་གུ་རུ་རིན་པོ་ཆེའི་ཐུགས་ཀར་
ཐིམ་པས་དབྱེར་མེད་རོ་གཅིག་ཏུ་གྱུར་པར་བསྒོམ།

(ཞིང་དམིགས་བསམ་བརྗོད་པ་དང་བྲལ་བའི་ངང་ལ་མཉམ་པར་བཞག་གོ།)

དེ་ལས་ལྡང་ནས།

༡ དཔལ་ལྡན་རྩ་བའི་བླ་མ་རིན་པོ་ཆེ།

༢ བདག་གི་སྙིང་གར་པདྨའི་གདན་བཞུགས་ལ།

༣ བཀའ་དྲིན་ཆེན་པོའི་སྒོ་ནས་རྗེས་བཟུངས་ཏེ།

༤ སྐུ་གསུང་ཐུགས་ཀྱི་དངོས་གྲུབ་སྩལ་དུ་གསོལ།

༡ དཔལ་ལྡན་བླ་མའི་རྣམ་པར་ཐར་པ་ལ།
༢ སྐད་ཅིག་ཙམ་ཡང་ལོག་ལྟ་མི་སྐྱེ་ཞིང་།
༣ ཅི་མཛད་ལེགས་པར་མཐོང་བའི་མོས་གུས་ཀྱིས།
༤ བླ་མའི་བྱིན་རླབས་སེམས་ལ་འཇུག་པར་ཤོག།

༡ སྐྱེ་བ་ཀུན་ཏུ་ཡང་དག་བླ་མ་དང་།
༢ འབྲལ་མེད་ཆོས་ཀྱི་དཔལ་ལ་ལོངས་སྤྱོད་ནས།
༣ ས་དང་ལམ་གྱི་ཡོན་ཏན་རབ་རྫོགས་ཏེ།
༤ རྡོ་རྗེ་འཆང་གི་གོ་འཕང་མྱུར་ཐོབ་ཤོག།།

བཅུ་པ་བསྔོ་བ་ནི།

༡ དགེ་བ་འདི་ཡིས་སྐྱེ་བོ་ཀུན།
༢ བསོད་ནམས་ཡེ་ཤེས་ཚོགས་རྫོགས་ཤིང་།
༣ བསོད་ནམས་ཡེ་ཤེས་ལས་བྱུང་བ།
༤ དམ་པ་སྐུ་གཉིས་ཐོབ་པར་ཤོག།

༡ འགྲོ་ཀུན་དགེ་བ་ཇི་སྙེད་ཡོད་པ་དང་།
༢ བྱས་དང་བྱེད་འགྱུར་དེ་བཞིན་བྱེད་པ་གང་།
༣ བཟང་པོ་ཇི་བཞིན་དེ་འདྲའི་ས་དག་ལ།
༤ ཀུན་ཀྱང་ཀུན་ནས་བཟང་པོར་རེག་གྱུར་ཅིག།

༡ འཇམ་དཔལ་དཔའ་བོས་ཇི་ལྟར་མཁྱེན་པ་དང་།

༢ ཀུན་ཏུ་བཟང་པོ་དེ་ཡང་དེ་བཞིན་ཏེ།

༣ དེ་དག་ཀུན་གྱི་རྗེས་སུ་བདག་སློབ་ཅིང་།

༤ དགེ་བ་འདི་དག་ཐམས་ཅད་རབ་ཏུ་བསྔོ།

༡ དུས་གསུམ་གཤེགས་པའི་རྒྱལ་བ་ཐམས་ཅད་ཀྱིས།

༢ བསྔོ་བ་གང་ལ་མཆོག་ཏུ་བསྔགས་པ་སྟེ།

༣ བདག་གི་དགེ་བའི་རྩ་བ་འདི་ཀུན་ཀྱང་།

༤ བཟང་པོ་སྤྱོད་ཕྱིར་རབ་ཏུ་བསྔོ་བར་བགྱི།

བཅུ་གཅིག་པ་སྨོན་ལམ་ཁྱད་པར་ནི།

༡ གང་དུ་སྐྱེས་པའི་སྐྱེ་བ་ཐམས་ཅད་དུ།

༢ མཐོ་རིས་ཡོན་ཏན་བདུན་ལྡན་ཐོབ་པར་ཤོག།

༣ སྐྱེས་མ་ཐག་ཏུ་ཆོས་དང་འཕྲད་གྱུར་ཅིང་།

༤ ཚུལ་བཞིན་བསྒྲུབ་པའི་རང་དབང་ཡོད་པར་ཤོག།

༥ དེར་ཡང་བླ་མ་དམ་པ་མཉེས་བྱེད་ཅིང་།

༦ ཉིན་དང་མཚན་དུ་ཆོས་ལ་སྤྱོད་པར་ཤོག།

༧ ཆོས་རྟོགས་ནས་ནི་སྙིང་པོའི་དོན་བསྒྲུབས་ཏེ།

༨ ཚེ་དེས་སྲིད་པའི་རྒྱ་མཚོ་བརྒལ་བར་ཤོག།

༩ སྲིད་པར་དམ་པའི་ཆོས་རབ་སྟོན་བྱེད་ཅིང་།

༡༠ གཞན་ཕན་བསྒྲུབ་ལ་སྐྱོ་ངལ་མེད་པར་ཤོག།

༡༡ རླབས་ཆེན་གཞན་དོན་ཕྱོགས་རིས་མེད་པ་ཡིས།

༡༢ ཐམས་ཅད་ཆབས་གཅིག་སངས་རྒྱས་ཐོབ་པར་ཤོག། ༎

ཅེས་རྫོགས་པ་ཆེན་པོ་ཀློང་ཆེན་སྙིང་ཐིག་གི་སྔོན་འགྲོའི་ངག་འདོན་ཁྲིགས་སུ་
བསྡེབས་པ་རྣམ་མཁྱེན་ལམ་བཟང་། འདི་ཉིད་རིག་འཛིན་འཇིགས་མེད་གླིང་
པ་སོགས་དམ་པ་དུ་མས་བཀའ་དྲིན་གྱིས་བསྐྱངས་ཤིང་། དམ་ཚིག་ལ་མོས་པ་
ཐོབ་པའི་སྟུགས་ཀྱི་རྣལ་འབྱོར་པ་ཆེན་པོ་འཇིགས་མེད་འཕྲིན་ལས་འོད་ཟེར་གྱིས་
བྲིས་པའི་དགེ་བས། རྗེས་འཇུག་རྣམས་ཀྱིས་བླ་མ་སངས་རྒྱས་སུ་མཐོང་འབྲས་
ཀྱིས། རང་རིག་ཀུན་ཏུ་བཟང་པོའི་རང་ཞལ་མངོན་དུ་གྱུར་ནས་འགྲོ་ཁམས་རྒྱ་
མཚོ་ལ་ཕན་པ་རྒྱུན་ཆད་མེད་པའི་རྒྱུར་གྱུར་ཅིག། ||